Literacy Skills

Grammar and punctuation

AGES 8–

TERM-BY-TERM PHOTOCOPIABLES

AUTHOR HUW THOMAS

EDITOR CLARE GALLAHER

ASSISTANT EDITOR CLARE MILLER

SERIES DESIGNER CLAIRE BELCHER

DESIGNER MARK UDALL

ILLUSTRATIONS TIM ARCHBOLD

Designed using Adobe Pagemaker

Published by Scholastic Ltd, Villiers House, Clarendon Avenue, Leamington Spa, Warwickshire CV32 5PR
Text © Huw Thomas

© 1999 Scholastic Ltd

7 8 9 0   5 6

British Library Cataloguing-in-Publication Data
A catalogue record for this book is available from the British Library.

ISBN 0-590-63650-2

Acknowledgements
The publishers gratefully acknowledge permission to reproduce the following copyright material:
Jackie Andrews for the retelling of the story 'The Elves and the Shoemaker' © 1999, Jackie Andrews, previously unpublished.
Houghton Mifflin Co, New York for 'Night Clouds' from *The Complete Poetical Works of Amy Lowell* © 1955 by Houghton Mifflin Co © renewed 1983 by Houghton Mifflin Co, Brinton P Roberts and G D'Andelot Belin Esq (1955, Houghton Mifflin Co).
Macmillan Children's Books for the use of quotes from the back cover of *Two Weeks with the Queen* by Morris Gleitzmann © 1990, Macmillan (1990, Piper).
The Observer for the use of an extract from the article 'Vieri picks lock then Italy shut door' from the issue of *The Observer* 28 June 1998 © 1998, The Observer.
Penguin Books Ltd and Benjamin Zephaniah for four lines from 'De Generation Rap' from *Talking Turkeys* by Benjamin Zephaniah. Text © 1994, Benjamin Zephaniah, typographical arrangement © 1994, The Point (1994, Viking); quotes from the back cover of *Nicobobinus* by Terry Jones © 1987, Penguin Books Ltd (1987, Puffin); an extract of text and an illustration from *It's Too Frightening For Me!* by Shirley Hughes. Text and Illustration © 1993, Shirley Hughes (1993, Viking).
Peters Fraser and Dunlop Group Ltd for the use of an extract from 'Boasts' by Michael Rosen from *Kingfisher Book of Children's Poetry* chosen by Michael Rosen © 1985, Michael Rosen (1985, Kingfisher).
Julia MacRae and Random House for the use of an extract twice and quotes from the back of the paperback from *Harvey Angell* by Diana Hendry © 1997, Diana Hendry (1997, Red Fox).
Scholastic Australia for the use of a text extract from *Dead Worried* by Moya Simons © 1996, Moya Simons (1996, Omnibus Books).
Scholastic Ltd for the use of 'Santa Fe' from *Mind Your Own Business* by Michael Rosen © 1996, Michael Rosen (1996, André Deutsch).
Sony Music Publishing for lines from the song 'You Gotta Be' © 1998, Des'ree Weekes/Ashley Ingram.
Walker Books Ltd for quotes from the back of *Granny* by Anthony Horowitz © 1995, Walker Books Ltd (1995, Walker Books).

Every effort has been made to trace copyright holders for the works reproduced in this book, and the publishers apologize for any inadvertent omissions.

Contents

Introduction

Welcome to grammar and punctuation

'As a writer I know that I must select studiously the nouns, pronouns, verbs, adverbs, etcetera, and by a careful syntactical arrangement make readers laugh, reflect or riot.'

Maya Angelou

The *Scholastic Literacy Skills: Grammar and punctuation* series equips teachers with resources and subject training enabling them to teach grammar and punctuation at Key Stage 2. The focus of the resource is on what is sometimes called *sentence-level* work, so called because grammar and punctuation primarily involve the construction and understanding of sentences.

Many teachers approach the teaching of grammar bringing with them a lot of past memories. Some will remember school grammar lessons as the driest of subjects, involving drills and parsing, and will wonder how they can make it exciting for their own class. At the other end of the spectrum, some will have received relatively little formal teaching of grammar at school. Recent research by the Qualifications and Curriculum Authority found a lack of confidence among Key Stage 2 teachers when it came to teaching sentence structure, commenting that:

'Where teachers were less confident, it tended to be because sentence structure had not formed part of their own education.'

(QCA, 1998, page 28)

In other words there are teachers who, when asked to teach clause structure or prepositions, feel at a bit of a loss. They are being asked to teach things they are not confident with themselves. Even worse, they think they should be confident in these things.

Grammar can evoke lethargy, fear, irritation, pedantry and despondency. Yet at the beginning of this introduction we have one of the greatest modern writers presenting her crafting of sentences as an exciting and tactical process that has a powerful effect on her readers. Can this be the grammar that makes teachers squirm or run?

The *Scholastic Literacy Skills: Grammar and punctuation* series

The *Scholastic Literacy Skills: Grammar and punctuation* series works from the premise that grammar and punctuation can be interesting and dynamic – but on one condition. The condition is that the teaching of these aspects of grammar must be related to *real texts* and *practical activities* that experiment with language, investigate the use of language in real contexts and find the ways in which grammar and punctuation are used in our day-to-day talk, writing and reading. The series is based upon five principles about the teaching of grammar:

1. Meaningful sentence-level work

In looking at how sentences are put together in a text, an appreciation of the function of that text is crucial. As children investigate the structure of sentences or the types of words they contain, they need to be aware of them as communicative acts; the purposes of the various pieces of writing considered in this resource play a crucial role in the activities. As children work through various aspects of *Grammar and punctuation*, teachers should reflect on how individual children are using their developing understanding of sentences in the rest of their written and spoken work.

2. Language from real life

As far as is possible, children need to work with language set in real-life contexts rather than always looking at contrived texts and exercises. Instead of made-up newspapers, for example, they need to look at extracts from the real thing. They need the encouragement to look at language in their environment, the books they enjoy and the things they and their peers say to one another. These are some of the most valuable resources available for language work because in using them children will apply what they learn to texts they know.

The *Scholastic Literacy Skills: Grammar and punctuation* series does contain a number of exercises in which sentences have been constructed purely to provide examples of the use of a particular type of word or punctuation mark. However, this is always complemented by more realistic uses of language. The aim is consistently to refer children to genuine texts extracted from real books and actual newspapers. For this reason the *Scholastic Literacy Skills: Grammar and punctuation* series asks children to work on grammar and punctuation using texts as diverse as fables, jokes, book blurbs, leaflets, children's own writing, comic stories, poems, scripts, comedy sketches, labels, classic poetry, texts in various dialects… in fact the mix is as rich and lively as the children's own language experiences should be. A flick through the photocopiable material in this book will show the commitment of the series to varied and interesting texts based on the conviction that relevant and appropriate texts will motivate children to learn about language.

3. Teachers as active participants

The 'rules' of grammar and punctuation are not static aspects of language; we are all continually revising and developing them. The most competent and experienced of writers can still find new and interesting features of these aspects of language and develop their own use of English. Because of this the *Scholastic Literacy Skills: Grammar and punctuation* series equips the teacher with subject knowledge, definitions and explanations as

preparation for the subject matter of each unit. It is important that, as far as is possible, teachers join in with activities. If, for example, an activity involves bringing a leaflet in from home and looking at the use of persuasive language, then everyone should take part. What many teachers have found is that grammar and punctuation can be great levellers. In other words, as children investigate these aspects of language, the teacher can join in and genuinely participate in developing his or her own use of English.

4. Structure is essential

While the *Scholastic Literacy Skills: Grammar and punctuation* series is full of interesting and lively material, it is underpinned by a clear and deliberate structure. The sentence-level aspects of English are so many and so varied that teaching them effectively demands a structured approach. The basic aim has been to provide a clearly structured resource that uses common sense and introduces features such as sentence structure and punctuation in ways that build continuity and progression into children's learning.

The half-term sections and units of each book are structured in a way that develops the teaching of grammar and punctuation in Key Stage 2 in England, Wales and Northern Ireland, and Levels C–E in Scotland. Care has been taken to encompass the National Literacy Strategy *Framework for Teaching* (DfEE, 1998), so that teachers following the strategy can use these books with the confidence that they are delivering all the appropriate sentence-level objectives for each year group.

5. Active enjoyment

This is not a book of basic drills. The *Scholastic Literacy Skills: Grammar and punctuation* series was put together in the knowledge that grammar and punctuation *can* be taught in a dry and dull way but with a commitment to do the complete opposite. With this in mind, the activities are constructed in a way that involves a lot of active investigative work and play with language.

The books provide a balanced 'diet' of exercises mixed with practical, hands-on activities, including researching language, recording and analysing speech, drama activities, games and advertising. The underlying premise is that language is interesting, that understanding it can be fascinating and that working with it can be fun.

Grammar and punctuation: do they matter?

Any introduction to the teaching of grammar and punctuation sets up a stall in the middle of one of the hottest debates in the teaching of English. For this reason it is necessary to say a few things about the usefulness and purpose of sentence-level teaching.

Background

There was a period from the 1960s to the 1980s when the teaching of grammar in particular and punctuation to a lesser extent was not in vogue. This was, in part, due to research projects in the 1960s that claimed to have shown the teaching of such aspects of English to be 'useless' and even 'harmful' (for example, Harris's research summarized in QCA, 1998). The Kingman Report in 1988 marked a change in this situation. After a period in which grammar had lain dormant, this report promoted the use of grammatical terminology in relevant contexts and recommended that all trainee teachers receive a large amount of 'direct tuition of knowledge about language' (HMSO, 1988, page 69).

A large portion of the Kingman Report was devoted to considering the talk and work of children. These were examined and the implicit linguistic knowledge in these activities was drawn out, such as the six-year-old whose writing demonstrated implicit understanding of subordinate clauses and qualifying phrases (HMSO, 1988, page 36). Taking the example of discussion about pronouns they made a comment that:

'Since… teacher and pupil need, in discussion, a word which refers to a class of terms (i.e. pronouns) there is no good reason not to use that term.'

(HMSO, 1988, page 13)

What Kingman raised was the usefulness of knowledge about language in the teaching of English.

Reasons for teaching grammar and punctuation

Grammar and punctuation are sometimes seen as symbols of a golden age when children were taught 'the basics'. This sort of talk has not served the subject well. It took some time for the Kingman recommendations to permeate into the English curriculum in a thorough and progressive way. It is crucial that, as teachers embark on the teaching of grammar and punctuation, they do so with a clear sense of exactly what it is these subjects will provide the learner with. The *Scholastic Literacy Skills: Grammar and punctuation* series is based on the following theoretical understanding of the value of teaching grammar and punctuation.

❑ Understanding and using terminology used to describe aspects of grammar and punctuation equips children with the vocabulary they need to discuss language. For example, it can be much easier to discuss the ambiguities that can surround the use of pronouns with children if they understand the term 'pronoun' and are beginning to use it to describe some of the words they use.

❑ Looking at aspects of sentence construction stimulates children to reflect on their own use of language. For example, many teachers try to discourage the overuse of the word 'and…' as in 'I went out and I saw my friend and we played in the park and we went to the shop and we bought…' and so on. Guiding children out of this overuse of 'and' is a task with which many teachers are familiar. It can be greatly enhanced by an understanding of certain aspects of grammar and punctuation such as how sentences break up a piece of writing so that it makes sense; other words and terms that can connect sentences and clauses together; ways in which sentences and clauses can be punctuated; and the functions performed by specific connecting words and phrases.

❑ There are links within the subject of English that make one aspect vital to the understanding of another. For example, the understanding of how certain texts address and persuade their readers involves an awareness of the concept of 'person' in pronouns and verbs. Another example is the way in which the use of the comma can depend on an understanding of how clauses function. Many aspects of grammar and punctuation play vital roles in other areas of English.

❑ Grammar and punctuation can provide a means of evaluating how effectively and clearly a spoken or written piece of language communicates. For example, the teacher who is exasperated by a child's constant use of the word 'nice' to describe everything he or she likes might find some work on adjectives steers the child towards new ways of describing.

❑ An appreciation of grammar and punctuation empowers children to make full use of the English language. Starting with simple sentences, children can move on to an understanding of features such as nouns, verbs, commas, clauses, adjectives and adverbs. Grammar and punctuation become the tools that enable children to explore new ways of expressing themselves in their writing.

❑ Linguistics, the study of language, is a subject in its own right. Looking at grammar and punctuation gives children their first encounters with this fascinating subject. The discussion of language features such as dialect words and expressions introduces children to the subject of sociolinguistics. This is the study of how language functions within society and it is just one example of the way in which the study of language can be an interesting subject in itself.

Working with *Scholastic Literacy Skills: Grammar and punctuation*
Unit structure

Each book in the *Scholastic Literacy Skills: Grammar and punctuation* series is broken up into six sections, each of which is structured to provide resources for a half-term. Within each section, material is gathered together to give a specific content to that half-term, indicated on the contents page. Each section contains two 'posters' that present some of the material covered over the half-term in an accessible form for reference. These are so named because it is recommended that they are enlarged to A3 size (or A2, using two A3 sheets) and placed on display while the units are undertaken. They can also be used as shared texts in reading activities as well as posters provided for reference in the classroom.

Each half-term section is split into five units, each dealing with a specific aspect of grammar or punctuation. Within each unit there are three photocopiables. These are prefaced by introductory material, structured under the following headings:

Objective: the learning objective(s) for the unit.

Language issues: explanatory material on the issues covered in the unit. These are predominantly focused on the subject matter of the unit and can provide clarification for the teacher, equipping him or her towards delivery of the unit.

Ways of teaching: notes on the teaching of the subject matter. This section can provide specific points about the approach to be adopted and the terminology to be used, and has a specific bearing upon the teaching of the unit.

About the activities: a note that clarifies any information the teacher may need for the unit. In some cases this is a full explanation of the activity; in others it is just a hint on the presentation of the subject matter.

Following up: optional activity suggestions to follow up the content of the unit. These can be specific activities but they can also be notes as to how the content of the unit can dovetail with other aspects of English.

Differentiation

The activities in each book are produced with the average ability of the relevant year group in mind. They draw upon the work of the National Literacy Project, a pilot project that led to the production of the National Literacy Strategy (DfEE, 1998). Differentiation should be possible within each unit in the following ways:

❑ *Providing support* in the way activities are staged. When, for example, there are three stages to an activity, the teacher can assist children who need support through one or more of the stages.

❑ *Reducing the amount of material.* If an activity asks children to complete a certain number of tasks, such as the ordering of ten mixed-up sentences, the teacher may reduce the number for a child needing such support.

❑ *Pre-selecting appropriate material* for investigative tasks. Many of the units ask children to find texts or try activities with sentences they find in the classroom. In such cases the teacher could direct children who would find this difficult to specified sentences or previously selected material.

❑ *Providing follow-up work.* More able children can benefit from being given one of the tasks under the heading 'Following up', extending their work based on the objective of the unit.

A 'resource', not a 'scheme'

The photocopiables in each book are a support for teaching. While they may carry notes to inform children, the actual teaching of the learning objective can only be achieved through discussion of the language issues supported by the use of the photocopiable sections. This takes us back to the idea of the teacher as an active participant. These materials are to be used by the class working in conjunction with the teacher and should support the teacher's explanation and discussion of the subject matter in each unit.

It should be stressed that *Scholastic Literacy Skills: Grammar and punctuation* does not intend to provide a scheme that children slavishly work their way through. It is a flexible teaching resource. While each book provides the subject matter appropriate to the age group at which it is aimed, the teacher will soon realize there is more material in each book than a class could be expected to cover in one year. The introductory pages at the start of each half-termly section and the language issues sections are there to enable teachers to select the photocopiable

page, poster, or activity from the 'Following up' section, that best supports their own planning, the needs of the class – and personal preferences.

Texts, texts and more texts!
Various activities call for a range of resources. Check each activity to see what is needed in the way of paper, scissors, glue and so on. The most valuable resource, however, is a rich variety of texts available for the children's use – collect together a truly mixed bag of old and new texts (familiar and unfamiliar), including leaflets, menus, newspapers, comics, letters, junk mail, posters… the broader the range the better!

Introduction to Ages 8–9
The thirty units comprising *Scholastic Literacy Skills: Grammar and punctuation, Ages 8–9* have as their objective a consolidation of various aspects of grammar and punctuation to which children will already have been introduced (such as verb tenses and adjectives), as well as an exploration of new subject matter such as adverbs and connectives. These are vital aspects of the child's knowledge of language.

These units also introduce punctuation that moves beyond the basics of capital letters and full stops, to introduce readers to colons and semicolons and the uses of the apostrophe.

For this age group, children are also encouraged to investigate how changes made to particular words (such as pluralizations and the adverbial ending *-ly*) indicate their grammatical function. There is a fair amount of terminology introduced (such as 'comparative' and 'superlative') and the teacher will need to decide which terms are vital for the children and in which cases they can learn the ideas without worrying too much about the specific terms used.

Verbs

Contents of Term 1a

Unit 1: **Verbs**	Revise and investigate verb tenses
Unit 2: **Tense and purpose**	Develop awareness of how tense relates to purpose and structure of text
Unit 3: **Verb power**	Identify and use powerful verbs
Unit 4: **Verbs in literature**	Identify and use powerful verbs
Unit 5: **Checking verbs**	Revise and investigate verb tenses Understand and use the term 'tense' Use tense as a test of whether a word is a verb or not

This half-term

The units in this half-term look at the tenses of verbs and at the range of verbs that can be used. They also look at the way verbs are matched to the context in which they are used, such as the link between a particular type of text and the verb tenses that will be used in it and the uses of verbs in literature.

Poster notes

Alternative verbs
As children look at the selection and effect of various verbs, this poster provides a basic thesaurus with which they can select the appropriate term for an action. It can be used as a tool for writing or as a way of spicing up sentences when redrafting.

Past and present tenses
This poster provides some examples of tense changes. It can be used as a teaching poster – if the columns are covered over in turn, children can be asked to supply past tenses for present tenses and vice versa.

Alternative verbs

look	say	walk	run
see	whisper	stroll	dart
peep	shout	pace	dash
regard	mumble	step	scarper
watch	announce	trudge	sprint
view	speak	shuffle	scramble
gaze	tell	amble	scurry
gape	remark	move	hurry
gawk	mention	march	race

find	hold	jump	make
discover	grip	bound	assemble
unearth	grasp	spring	create
disclose	seize	hop	construct
acquire	grab	leap	produce
recover	clutch	pounce	manufacture
spot	possess	bounce	build
learn	clasp	vault	generate
notice	squeeze	lurch	fashion

Past and present tenses

Past	Present
bought	buy
saw	see
went	go
jumped	jump
opened	open
told	tell
found	find
heard	hear
stopped	stop
changed	change
knew	know
left	leave
showed	show
walked	walk
wrote	write
thought	think
turned	turn
asked	ask

Verbs

Objective
Revise and investigate verb tenses

Language issues
Tense shows the timing of a verb. It is the way a verb changes to show whether an action happened in the present ('I run') or the past ('I ran'). The word alters to denote when something happens.

In the English language there are two simple tenses – the present tense ('I walk') and the past tense ('I walked'). For these two tenses the verb itself can alter. The future tense is made in a compound form. This means another word is added to set a verb in the future, so in the above examples the simple present has the word 'will' added. This creates the compound forms 'will run' and 'will walk'.

Ways of teaching
The activities focus on spoken sentences. They look at the type of things children say and ask them to reflect on the tenses they are using. This unit should involve a lot of discussion, with groups analysing examples from their own language use.

About the activities
Photocopiable: Past, present or future
This activity revises the three simple tense forms. Ask the children to cut out the sentences, then encourage them to say the sentences out loud before sorting them into past, present and future tenses. They may want to make up some slips of their own, recording additional sentences that can be spoken aloud, then placing them in the correct group.

Photocopiable: Change the tense
Ask the children to choose eight sentences from the ones they have worked with on photocopiable page 14. Explain that each sentence should be written in the correct box, then written out again for the other two tenses. Some children may need to be directed towards particular sentences that gave them a challenge or stimulated their thinking in the earlier task.

Photocopiable: Using tenses
By using verbs in their tenses in this activity, the children can develop their understanding of how the tenses feature in certain types of sentence and the way the form of the verb indicates its tense. As an extra challenge, the children could try including more than one of the verbs shown in a sentence.

Following up
Role-play: In a group of four, two of the children in the group can listen to the other two acting out a conversation. It could be about things they enjoy or places they have visited. As they speak, the listeners make notes of the different tenses used. This will usually lead to the two role-players steering the conversation around the tenses and even pausing while notes are made, but it will still provide an insight into the use of tenses at different points in a conversation.

Spelling: As children engage in the activities in this unit, they may begin to comment on the spelling patterns evident in the various tenses. These can be highlighted and irregular verbs can also be noted.

Past, present or future

❑ Cut out the sentences. Say them aloud, then sort them into three piles.

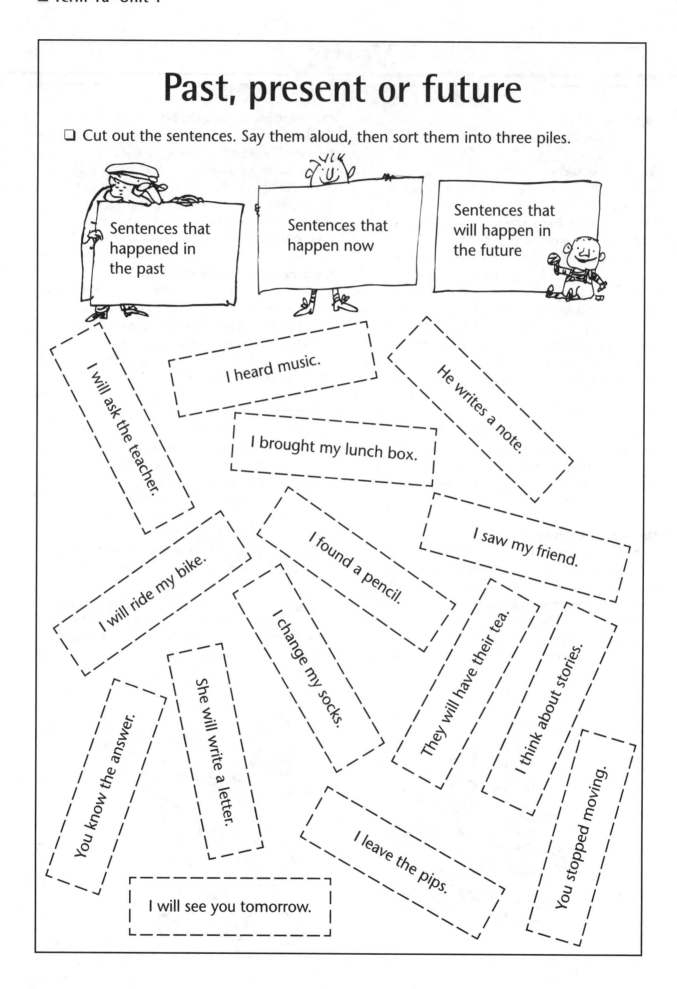

Sentences that happened in the past

Sentences that happen now

Sentences that will happen in the future

I will ask the teacher.

I heard music.

He writes a note.

I brought my lunch box.

I saw my friend.

I found a pencil.

I will ride my bike.

I change my socks.

They will have their tea.

I think about stories.

You know the answer.

She will write a letter.

You stopped moving.

I leave the pips.

I will see you tomorrow.

Change the tense

	past	present	future
1	I thought about stories.	I think about stories.	I will think about stories.
2			
3			
4			
5			
6			
7			
8			

Using tenses

❏ Look at these verbs.

ran   found   said

make   find

run   says

make   made

❏ Try to write **eight** sentences, each one containing a different verb chosen from the box.

1 _____

_____

2 _____

_____

3 _____

_____

4 _____

_____

5 _____

_____

6 _____

_____

7 _____

_____

8 _____

_____

Tense and purpose

Objective
Develop awareness of how tense relates to purpose and structure of text

Language issues
Different tenses are commonly used in different types of writing. A weather report will set sentences in the predicted future. A diary will usually record events that have happened in the past.

The recount of events in a narrative will tend to be written in the past tense (for example, 'I walked out onto the moor in the darkness…'). Explanatory reports are often in the present tense (for example, a house survey might state, 'The ground floor is in a good state of repair…'). Forecasts and predictions will be written in the future tense (for example, 'It will be showery at first…').

These are general rules. There are exceptions, such as narratives written in the present tense, but an understanding of the varied tenses used in different types of writing provides an insight into various text types. After all, it is obvious that a forecast, whether it is about the weather or the outcome of a football game, will be written in the future tense.

Ways of teaching
As children undertake these activities, it needs to be stressed that the text extracts are not just examples of the tenses at work. Throughout their work in this unit, draw the children's attention to the types of texts they are analysing. For instance, as they look at tenses in a magazine, they should be encouraged to look at different examples at home – they may find a present-tense report of facts about a film star, for example. As they provide their own examples of the types of text dealt with in this unit, the objectives in the activities can be applied to their own examples.

About the activities
Photocopiable: Write start
Ask the children to think ahead to the type of writing they will be doing in each of the three sections of the sheet – whether it will need to be written in the past tense, the present tense or the future tense. It is important that the three examples are written in close proximity to each other, to reinforce the differences in the tenses. Follow the activity with a plenary discussion, focusing on the thoughts the children had about the opening lines they were writing – the verbs they used and the reasons they used particular tenses.

Photocopiable: Tense finding
Collect together a variety of texts which the children can use for this activity. Newspapers and magazines will have suitable examples of the uses of different tenses, in contexts such as recipes and news stories.

Photocopiable: Magazine extracts
These example extracts show the way different texts use certain tenses. To give the activity a more contemporary slant, they can be supplemented by extracts from a current pop magazine. The children can analyse the tenses used in the texts and reflect on how they suit the purpose of the writing.

Following up
Reword the text: A number of the texts looked at in this activity could be reworded. Ask the children to change the tenses of sentences, for example they could rework a forecast into the past tense. This will often demonstrate just how much the tense supports the purpose of the original text.

Television excerpts: Tape-record three five-minute excerpts from the television. Examples could include a block of adverts, a short scene from a soap opera, a part of a children's information programme. When the children watch the excerpts ask them to listen carefully to try to find examples of the different tenses used in each of them.

Write start

❑ In these boxes write some opening lines for:

a diary extract about things that happened yesterday at school	a recipe for making toast or a cup of tea
a plan for what you will do in your next school holiday	❑ Look at the verbs you have used in each piece of writing. Fill in the grid.

Type of writing	Tense used
diary	
recipe	
holiday plan	

Tense finding

❑ Write down some sentences from the text you have been given. Look carefully at the tenses of the verbs.

Sample sentences

| The main tense in this text is | Why is this the common tense? |

The main tense in this text is

the _____ tense.

Why is this the common tense?

Magazine extracts

❏ Here are some extracts from a pop magazine. Pick out verbs and verb phrases with a highlighter pen. Note down the main tense used in each extract.

Queen Sweep

Pop group Sweeper flew in to London this week to receive their 'London Hits' award for best group. They also won the award for 'Best song' and came second in the 'Best video' award. But the band were more interested in other things. 'We wanted to see the Queen,' lead singer Sam told reporters. 'Yeh! We thought it would be cool and that she'd pop into the party. She probably went to the wrong place.'

main tense:

Widdering Heights

The news is out. Singer Phil Widders, pop's wild child, is scared of something. Phil tells us he hates tall buildings. 'I hate heights,' he says, 'but it is a strange sort of fear. I can happily stand on a tall building. I hate it when I stand outside one and look up at the top. It terrifies me.'
Hmmmmm.

main tense:

Buzz's new single, 'Melting'

Pop group Buzz have another hit with this one. Many say it is their best song ever. It features in the hit film 'Slides' and includes guitarist Matt doing a violin solo!

main tense:

New single from Mice Girls

Record shops will need space outside the doors on 14 July. The new Mice Girls single will be released on that date. The girls will fly into London for the release and will appear on the roof of 'Majestic Records' in the city, where they will perform the single for fans.

main tense:

Verb power

Objective
Identify and use powerful verbs

Language issues
Verb choice can be an important feature in the composition of a piece of writing. If our entrance into the room is recorded as 'sauntering into the room' this conjures up a very different picture from us 'storming into the room'.

If you take a particular sentence, there may be a verb that does not fit in with the tone of what is being expressed, for example, 'I stormed gently into the room.' While this type of incongruous verb can sound odd, it can also be used to the children's advantage as a way of making a sentence more striking and interesting. Also, some verbs are more specific than others. Stating 'I went into the room' is more open to a variety of interpretations than 'I fell into the room'.

There are some verbs that have particular connotations. They are connected with other experiences the hearer or reader of a text may have had. When we read of a politician 'slithering' to his party leader, we picture the sort of creature we usually associate with the verb 'slithering'.

Ways of teaching
Exploring this area of language with children involves looking at the possible verbs that can fit into a sentence and analysing selected examples. The activities encourage children to reflect on particular verb choices and to look for alternative words that can work in a particular way.

About the activities
Photocopiable: Choose a different verb
Looking at the atmosphere and setting of the passage, children can use words from the verb box to develop it. They may suggest some interesting combinations of words (for example, 'The tree ruffled in the wind').

There are more verbs suggested than there are words to be changed in the story, so children should not be under any pressure to find correct solutions in this task. They are being encouraged to experiment with possibilities. Indeed, a diversity of results makes the activity more worthwhile.

Photocopiable: Verb changes
Children can use this photocopiable sheet to record the changes made to the passage in 'Choose a different verb'. Alternatively, they can use the grid as a way of reviewing another piece of writing in which they have altered the verbs, using it as a means of reflecting on their own story writing.

Photocopiable: Possibilities
As adults write, they often stop to consider the best word to use in a particular situation. They weigh up the tactfulness and power of particular words. In this set of verb choices, children are encouraged to consider some of the verbs that could complete a sentence, collecting three possibilities for the same space in a sentence. Once they have finished the activity, they could compare their selected verbs with those that their friends chose and record next to each sentence any interesting possibilities they missed.

Following up
Thesauruses: Ask the children to use thesauruses to collate lists of alternative ways of denoting particular actions or happenings. They can also refer to the examples on the 'Alternative verbs' poster on page 11.

Verb-power list: Children can make lists of particularly powerful verbs they encounter in their reading. These lists could be used to compile an edited whole-class verb list of the best verbs that have been found.

Right verb in the right place: Find out, as a class, how different types of verbs are used in different contexts. For example, how do verbs that are used when the children are talking in the playground differ from verbs that are used in a letter to parents from the headteacher?

Choose a different verb

❏ Read this piece of writing. Find the verbs in it and try to improve them. Choose words from the lists and write the new words above the ones in the passage (cross out the words you are replacing).

crept	moaned	fled	spied
squealed	ruffled	pushed	whistled
whispered	banged	smashed	stepped
swung	swayed	leaped	wheeled
clattered	stuffed	fumbled	padded
swept	bounded	searched	hurried

The postwoman walked up to the creepy house. The tree moved in the wind.

The shutters closed together in the icy gust. The wind went through the

chimney pots. A cat went up the path. It jumped through the window. The

postwoman looked for the right letter. Inside

the house the cat pushed a vase off the table.

The vase broke on the floor. The postwoman

put the letter through the letter box.

She turned around to go. The cat saw the

crack of light from the door. The door moved

open. "Eeeeeek!" the hinges went.

The postwoman ran.

Verb changes

❑ Look at a piece of text in which you have changed the verbs. In this table record the original verb and the new verb you have chosen.

Original verb	My verb	Why is mine better?

Possibilities

❏ For each of the sentences below, list **three** possible verbs. Try to think of some powerful ones or some unusual ones.

The dog | ran / fled / leapt | from the burning house.

I | | round my room to find shoes.

Our baby | | because he was hungry.

The spaceship | | into space.

The thief | | when he saw the police car.

A firework | | in the sky.

The mountain climber | | onto the ledge.

My gran | | when she is in a bad mood.

The monster | | out of the cave.

I dropped a glass and it | | .

Verbs in literature

Objective
Identify and use powerful verbs

Language issues
Stylistics is the study of language in literature. It looks at how features of the language of a text relate to the meaning a reader draws from it. One interesting vein for exploration in this subject is the use of unusual combinations of words to create images. A metaphor involves one thing being described in terms of another, something with which it is not normally associated. Hence when a character in Shakespeare's *Romeo and Juliet* says, 'Come, we burn daylight, ho!' he conjures up an image, using the verb 'burn' to describe the using up of daylight.

Ways of teaching
Literature can provide a rich resource for developing children's awareness of powerful verb uses. In the activities in this unit children either encounter or create interesting uses of verbs. The pieces of literature are selected for the examples they contain of interesting and effective uses of verbs.

About the activities
Photocopiable: Fill the gaps
This activity uses a cloze exercise; the extract is taken from *Harvey Angell* by Diana Hendry (Red Fox) – see below. It can be done in two stages. Initially children can be asked to have a go at thinking of possible verbs that could be used in the text, filling in the spaces in pencil. If you then reveal the verbs used by the author, writing

---

*Henry **zapped** his alarm clock very quickly before it could **wake** Aunt Agatha. He **lay** still, listening. A sleepy silence **held** the house only **interrupted** by the occasional snorting snore from Aunt Agatha's room. Then there was movement! Creaks on the stairs! The sound of someone **whistling** in the kitchen. Harvey Angell was up and about...*

*Henry **slid** out of bed, **pulled** on his jeans and shirt and **waited**. He would **wait** until he **heard** the front door close, then he would **count** twenty, then he would **be** off, **following** Harvey Angell. Henry's mouth **felt** very dry. He **wished** he could **go** into the kitchen for a drink of water.*

---

them on a flip chart in random order, the children can try to see where they could fit. Then by comparing their choices with the original, it will be seen how verbs can be used in interesting and powerful ways.

Photocopiable: Different ways of saying
The powerful use of verbs in figurative and imaginative language is explored through this activity. Children can complete these sentences in any number of ways; they are deliberately given more words than there are spaces, so that they will be able to generate interesting and imaginative combinations, for example 'Raindrops dodged down the window pane'.

Photocopiable: Night clouds
Through this activity children explore the creative edge of language, looking at the use of verbs to denote the actions of the moonlit clouds across the night sky. It takes them beyond a straightforward identification of the verbs in the poem to a consideration of the effect of the verbs used.

Following up
Text verbs: Ask the children to look through a story or a poem and list some of the verbs they think are particular to that text. For example, in Maurice Sendak's *Where the Wild Things Are* (Bodley Head) Max *makes* mischief, he *sails* away on a boat, he *stares* into the eyes of the wild things. The verbs take on a particular association with the story.

Unusual combinations: Ask the children to look at a particular action, such as a cat rubbing against its owner's leg. They can consider the usual verbs for the action and then try out some unusual combinations (such as 'The cat swam against its owner's leg'), seeing the effects that a more imaginative choice of verb makes.

Collecting combinations: Particularly effective uses of powerful verbs can be recorded on a chart or in a small book. Ask the children to keep a look out for them in their reading and to jot down interesting examples, building up an enriched collection of alternative and powerful verb uses.

Fill the gaps

Harvey Angell is the story of a strange character, Harvey, who comes to live at the sad house of Henry and his Aunt Agatha. Henry is fascinated by Harvey and wants to know where he goes, very early each morning.
In this extract he decides to follow him.

❑ Read the passage and guess what the missing verbs could be.

Henry _____ his alarm clock very quickly before it could _____ Aunt

Agatha. He _____ still, listening. A sleepy silence _____ the house only

_____ by the occasional snorting snore from Aunt Agatha's room. Then

there was movement! Creaks on the stairs! The sound of someone _____

in the kitchen. Harvey Angell was up and about...

Henry _____ out of bed, _____ on his jeans and shirt and _____.

He would _____ until he _____ the front door close, then he would

_____ twenty, then he would _____ off, _____ Harvey Angell.

Henry's mouth _____ very dry. He _____ he could _____ into the

kitchen for a drink of water.

Diana Hendry

Different ways of saying

Metaphors involve using words to describe things they do not usually describe. If we say 'Leo is confused',

we could take the word 'drowning', which is usually associated with being in water,

and make an interesting image, 'Leo was drowning in confusion'.

❏ Cut out the verbs. See how many are suitable for each of the spaces. Write down some of the interesting sentences you make using different verbs.

swam	barked	dodged	smiled	flew	galloped	sidled
splattered	scuttled	screamed	slithered	slouched	stretched	hurtled

The cat	in the streetlight.
The runner	round the track.
My sister	into school.
The old man	with laughter.
Raindrops	down the window pane.
A mouse	round the pipes.
The sun	on the field.
A football	through the window.

Night clouds

The white mares of the moon rush along the sky

Beating their golden hoofs upon the glass Heavens;

The white mares of the moon are all standing on their hind legs

Pawing at the green porcelain doors of the remote Heavens.

Fly, mares!

Strain your utmost,

Scatter the milky dust of stars,

Or the tiger sun will leap upon you and destroy you

With one lick of his vermilion tongue.

Amy Lowell (1874–1925)

❑ Look at the verbs in the poem. What sort of action or happening do they make you think of? Write some notes about them on a separate sheet of paper.

Checking verbs

Objective
Revise and investigate verb tenses
Understand and use the term 'tense'
Use tense as a test of whether a word is a verb or not

Language issues
The question 'What is a verb?' will often be met with the reply 'A doing word'. There's a lot in that definition, but it can fail to account for verbs such as 'think' and 'know'. There are verbs in which the subject is not doing anything but has something done to it ('We were robbed'). There's also the fact that sentences can contain verb phrases, a set of words that denote the action or happening in the sentence (for example, 'We were being robbed'). One indication that a word is a verb is whether or not it can change tense. Verbs alter their form to account for the time at which the action or occurrence took place. This is something that can set them apart from other words.

Ways of teaching
In this unit children encounter words which can feature as verbs or other types of word in a given context (for example, 'hand' is a verb in 'Hand over the jewels!' and a noun in 'I cut my hand'). The tense test – that is, does the verb alter its form? – will help them to figure out which word in the sentence functions as a verb. In the first exercise they are asked to consider the conventional phrasing of a sentence and readjust it accordingly. Here again, tense proves critical.

About the activities
Photocopiable: Change the verb
Children will need to say the sentences aloud, sometimes saying them a few times as they rework them to natural language. Different children may make different changes to the sentences to make them sound right. The most natural change to 'When I went on the train I leave my umbrella' would be 'When I went on the train I left my umbrella'. However, a child might change it to the grammatically consistent 'When I go on the train I leave my umbrella'. This raises questions as to why anyone would deliberately lose an umbrella, but any variations like this in the results of this activity can be compared and discussed as alternative ways of reworking the tense.

Photocopiable: Tense test
One way to encourage children to change the tense in the sentences is to start by saying them aloud and

adding the word 'Yesterday', 'Today' or 'Tomorrow' to the beginning (for example, 'Yesterday the children laughed when the clown fell over'). They can then say the sentence using the alternative starter word ('Tomorrow the children will…') and rework the sentence accordingly, finding the words they alter – the verbs.

Photocopiable: Lend a hand
Children consider the different verbs and nouns in sentences such as 'Behind the cupboard I *find* lost toys' and 'She made a *find* in the cupboard'. They can also look at the links between these words. Point out that in sentences where the bold word is a noun they will be able to identify one of the other words in the sentence as a verb.

Following up
Tense test: Children can apply the tense test to a number of sentences to try finding verbs. For example, if they encounter a picture labelled 'A ship in a stormy sea' and add 'Yesterday' or 'Today' to the beginning, none of the words change, demonstrating that the string of words lacks a verb.

Making 'Lend a hand' sentences: Invite the children to try creating their own sentences containing words that can function either as verbs or as other types of words. A good starting point for this would be to seek out words which function as nouns that, in an alternative context, can act as verbs.

Verbless text: Ask the children to look out for verbless texts. These could include signs ('Sale. Low prices all day') or counting posters ('One smiling bullfrog, two happy hippos…'), for example.

Change the verb

❑ Change the verb in each of these sentences so that it makes sense. Think about the tense of the verb. The first one is done for you.

I found the shoe I lose.

I found the shoe I lost.

Last week I see my aunty when she cycles to our house.

Tomorrow we will go to the shop and bought some new shoes.

When I went on the train I leave my umbrella.

Every time we do PE I jumped off the wall bars.

We started a game of football then we stop when the bell ring.

We will turn off the TV because there was nothing on.

I write a letter and then I posted it.

My brother wakes up late and rushed to school.

I knew a game so I teach it to my friends.

Tense test

❑ The **tense test** can show whether a particular word is a verb. Look at this sentence.

I saw a saw.

❑ Say the sentence in a different tense.

I see a saw.

The word that changes tense is a verb.

I (see) a saw.

Sometimes words look like verbs but are actually nouns.

❑ Look at these sentences and find which words are used as a verb.

When I play football I run very fast.

Verbs	Changed tense
play	played
run	ran

The toffee is sticky so we chew it a lot.

Verbs	Changed tense

The children laughed when the clown fell over.

Verbs	Changed tense

Our teacher sits and listens to our moans about school.

Verbs	Changed tense

We went on a hunt and found some lost treasure.

Verbs	Changed tense

I go to the shop and buy a chew.

Verbs	Changed tense

On Saturday we will shop for shoes and buy ones we like.

Verbs	Changed tense

I made a promise and I kept it.

Verbs	Changed tense

Lend a hand

Some words can appear as verbs or other types of word. The word **try** is a verb in this sentence.

> *I try to finish all my work.*

It is a noun in this sentence:

> *Have a try at doing this.*

❑ Look at these sentences and sort them into two sets: those in which the highlighted word is a verb; those in which the highlighted word is not a verb. Tick the correct column. You may want to use the tense test to find the verbs.

	Verb	Not a verb
Behind the cupboard I **find** lost toys.		
She made a **find** in the cupboard.		
When we do writing I **hand** out the books.		
You raise your **hand** when you have a question.		
At the **start** of the race we waited to go.		
We **start** school at nine o'clock.		
I went through the **open** door.		
In summer I **open** all my windows.		
My dad **cut** my hair.		
We threw **cut** grass at each other.		
The children make up a **show** for their parents.		
At Open Evening we **show** our families our work.		
I check my **change** before I leave the shop.		
Our teachers **change** the timetable.		
I had an interesting **thought** and wrote it down.		
I **thought** I saw a flying saucer!		

Adverbs, commas and sentences

Contents of Term 1b

Unit 1: **Identifying adverbs**	Learn to identify adverbs, noticing where they occur in sentences and how they are used to qualify the verbs
Unit 2: **The 'ly' suffix**	Identify common adverbs with 'ly' suffix
Unit 3: **Classifying adverbs**	Collect and classify examples of adverbs
Unit 4: **Changing adverbs**	Investigate the effects of substituting adverbs in particular contexts
Unit 5: **Commas and sentences**	Practise the use of commas, separating grammatical boundaries within sentences

This half-term

The main focus for this half-term is on adverbs. Children look at the function they perform and the way they can be recognized. They also collect them and alter them. The final unit looks at the specific use of the comma to demarcate grammatical boundaries within sentences.

Poster notes

Adjectives to adverbs
The way adjectives can be turned into adverbs, looked at in Unit 2, provides a useful spelling lesson. However, it also helps children to identify adverbs. Once they have grasped this aspect of grammar, they will be able to turn adjectives they know into adverbs.

Sentences and clauses
The way clauses are structured is a complex idea. This poster gives a clear image of how commas are used in sentences. The inserted clause is known as a relative clause, providing extra information about the noun.

Adjectives to adverbs

The usual way of making an adverb out of an adjective

is to add **ly**.

If the adjective ends in **y**,

change the **y** to **i** before
adding **ly**.

How would you change these?

sad   **quick**   **angry**   **sleepy**

Sentences and clauses

When two clauses

> *I like coffee*

> *You like tea*

meet in the same sentence,

> *I like coffee   You like tea*

a comma can separate them.

> *I like coffee, You like tea*

Commas can make space for clauses

> *who lives next door*
>
> *Mr Carter   mended our cooker*

inside sentences.

> *Mr Carter, who lives next door, mended our cooker.*

No problem

Identifying adverbs

Objective
Learn to identify adverbs, noticing where they occur in sentences and how they are used to qualify the verbs

Language issues
Adverbs modify verbs. They are the words or phrases in a sentence that say something about the action or happening described by the verb.
A sentence could just state:
Albert collapsed.
It could say something about the manner in which he did this:
Albert suddenly collapsed.
It could say where:
Albert suddenly collapsed on the floor.
It could say when:
This morning Albert suddenly collapsed on the floor.
These additions are adverbs – words modifying the verb.

Ways of teaching
Once children have a grasp of the function of verbs in a sentence they can begin to see how the adverbs modify the verbs. In the activities in this unit, the children look for words and phrases that tell the reader or listener more about the verbs.

About the activities
Photocopiable: How verbs happen
By looking at the words that modify the verbs in the sentences, the children should begin to understand the type of word or phrase that constitutes an adverb. Because the term 'adverb' covers a range of different types of modifier, the exercise has drawn on various ways in which a verb can be qualified. Stress to the children that they are looking for words or phrases that could be removed from the sentence without impairing the sense. They are also looking for anything that says something about the verb.

Photocopiable: Tell us more
This activity gives children an opportunity to experiment with their own production of adverbs. They could use the poster on photocopiable page 34 for reference, as well as a list of adverbs compiled by the whole class.

Photocopiable: Action and manner
This is a game to play in a large group. Photocopy the sheet onto card and cut out the cards. Put the children into small teams of two or three. Place the cards face down in two piles. Each team takes turns to select an 'action' card and a 'manner' card. They then mime the action and the manner in which it is done. The other children have to guess the action and the manner. Stress that the actions are to be mimed, and that speaking is not allowed.

Following up
Adverb mimes: The children can build on the 'Action and manner' activity by performing other actions in the manner of the adverbs on the cards. As their stock of adverbs develops they can create new 'manner' cards to modify the actions.

Comic pages: Provide the children with comics and ask them to make a list of the pictorial representations of actions that they can see on the pages. They can then use adverbs to describe the manner in which each action is being done.

Modify it: Invite the children to produce simple sentences such as the 'Albert collapsed' examples. Can they think of words that they could add to their starter phrase (for example, 'Albert slowly, quietly and foolishly collapsed'), gradually producing a lengthy sentence with a list of adverbs modifying the verb?

How verbs happen

❑ Look at each of these examples of things people say and find the verbs (the actions or happenings) and the words that tell us about the verb.
For example:

The boy quickly ran downstairs.

Verb	Words about the verb
ran	quickly, downstairs

We played well on the muddy field.

Verb	Words about the verb

Screw the bottle top on firmly after use.

Verb	Words about the verb

I planted the seeds outside.

Verb	Words about the verb

Today we will sing pleasantly.

Verb	Words about the verb

Listen carefully to the answerphone.

Verb	Words about the verb

Tell us more

A sentence could say
Lucy fell.

It could also say
Today Lucy suddenly fell off her chair.

❏ In the boxes draw pictures of people (or animals or monsters!) doing things. Write a sentence to explain the picture. Use an adverb to give a clear description of what is happening.

Picture	Picture	Picture
Sentence Daniel wrote his story quickly.	Sentence	Sentence
Picture	Picture	Picture
Sentence	Sentence	Sentence

Action and manner

action taking a dog for a walk	**manner** slowly
action playing the piano	**manner** quickly
action pouring and eating breakfast cereal	**manner** happily
action mixing paints	**manner** pompously
action getting dressed	**manner** miserably
action meeting friends	**manner** sneakily
action catching a bus	**manner** nervously

The 'ly' suffix

Objective
Identify common adverbs with 'ly' suffix

Language issues
Most adverbs are adverbs of manner. They explain how something was done. The majority of these adverbs are made by altering an adjective, either adding 'ly' to the end:

sad → *sadly*

or, if the adjective ends in 'y', changing the 'y' to 'i' then adding 'ly'.

happy → *happily*

As with most spelling rules, there are exceptions to the rule, such as the word 'fast'. It can function as an adjective or it can remain the same to make an adverb:

fast talk

talk fast

However, as spelling rules go, the 'ly' one acts as an important guide in working with adverbs.

Ways of teaching
As with any spelling rule, children need to learn the rule while also understanding the fact that there are exceptions. In these activities children encounter the 'ly' rule and also meet some of the exceptions. It is therefore important that they keep the overall definition of an adverb in mind and don't just rely on the 'ly' ending to discern which words fall into this class.

About the activities
Photocopiable: Create the adverb
This activity asks children to apply the 'ly' rule to a range of adjectives. Before they start to work on the sheet, remind them of the function of an adjective and the important link between an action and the word (the adverb) that describes the action. Explain the activity by working on a few examples together on a flip chart, changing a phrase containing an adjective to a sentence using an adverb formed from the adjective; encourage the children to think of a context in which a particular action could occur – for example, the phrase 'a soft step' could become the sentence 'The burglar stepped softly'.

Photocopiable: Find the adverb
Review the nature and function of adverbs with the children undertaking this activity, and encourage them to refer to the poster on photocopiable page 34. The sentences contain exceptions to the 'ly' rule alongside adverbs that conform to it. The exceptions may cause some discussion and debate.

Photocopiable: Making and using
Explain to the children that after reading the definitions of the adjectives and writing down the adverbs, they need to think of an action for each one that could be performed in a way that would merit the description given in the definition. They should then make up a sentence using the adverb.

Following up
Links: Encourage the children to develop the habit of looking at adverbs to work out what the linked adjectives could be, and vice versa. In some cases adjectives do not have linked adverbs, for example adjectives that describe colour, such as 'red'. What could it mean to perform an action 'redly'? What about the adjective 'fishy'? What sort of actions are done 'fishily'? Let the activity lead in to children inventing new adverbs.

Dictionary hunt: Ask the children to search through a dictionary, listing unfamiliar adjectives, then finding or forming the linked adverbs.

Create the adverb

Adverbs are often made by adding **ly** to an adjective.

If the adjective ends in **y**, the **y** is changed to an **i** before adding the **ly**.

A quick paint.   *She painted the wall quickly.*

❑ Write a short sentence for each of the actions. Add **ly** to the adjective (the bold word) to make your adverb.

Phrase with adjective	Use the adverb
an **immediate** cry	She cried immediately when she hurt herself.
a **sudden** flash	
an **angry** shout	
a **sweet** sing	
a **quick** jump	
a **strong** swim	
a **creepy** look	
a **quiet** whisper	
a **sharp** turn	

Find the adverb

❏ Look at the sentences and circle the adverb.
(Warning 1: some adverbs don't end in **ly**.)
(Warning 2: not every word that ends in **ly** is an adverb.)

❏ Fill in the table to show the adverbs you found and the verbs they describe.

	Adverb	Verb it describes
A fly buzzed briskly around the room.	briskly	buzzed
Don't talk fast because it confuses me.		
You ran well and won the race.		
The dragon fought bravely with the monster.		
The plane flew low.		
Joe woke early and read his book.		
We quickly emptied the smelly old bottle.		
Dad accidentally dropped the telly.		
Lou pulled hard and my welly came off.		
We walked slowly into the temple.		
Leon slipped late into the silent classroom.		

Making and using

❑ Look at the list of adjectives (describing words) and their dictionary definitions. Make adverbs out of the adjectives by adding **ly**.
If they end in a **y**, change the **y** to an **i** before adding **ly**.

❑ Use the new adverb in a made-up sentence.

Adjective and definition	Adverb	Sentence
abominable awful, monstrous, horrible	→ abominably	The boy behaved abominably, throwing plates around the room.
bashful timid or shy, easily embarrassed	→	
cautious wary, taking care	→	
despondent sad, 'down in the dumps'	→	
entire complete, finished	→	
forthright honest, up front, stating something clearly	→	
gloomy miserable, with gloom	→	
humorous funny, making people laugh	→	
impetuous acting in a hasty way, without thinking things through	→	
jealous wanting what another has	→	

Classifying adverbs

Objective
Collect and classify examples of adverbs

Language issues
The term 'adverb' covers a large group of words and phrases. These can be sorted according to the different functions they perform. The main groups of adverbs are those that explain:

Manner: how a verb happened, for example 'He ran *quickly*'.

Place: where a verb happened, for example 'He ran *upstairs*'.

Time: when a verb happened, for example '*Later*, he ran'.

These are the main categories of adverb, though there are others. There are also groups of adverbs that tend to modify particular verbs. There are verbs that particularly relate to the speed at which things happened (for example, 'quickly', 'slowly') and the attitude in which actions were performed (for example, 'happily', 'miserably').

Ways of teaching
Children can explore the groups of adverbs as a way of extending and developing their grasp of the function of adverbs. Through differentiating between different functions, children investigate various types of adverb. The activities in this unit look at the points at which adverbs are used and encourage the children to select the appropriate words to perform this function.

A note of caution: adverbs can be overused. The activities are intended to prompt children to use and understand adverbs, but there is a need to guard against overuse.

About the activities
Photocopiable: Sort the adverbs
Three broad categories of adverb are presented: adverbs of manner, time and place. Encourage the children to look at the adverb as an answer to a question about the action. What question could it be answering? Does the adverb answer 'How?' something was done, or 'When?' or 'Where?'

Photocopiable: Adverb families
This activity focuses on adverbs that can be linked to certain types of action or happening. When the children have completed each 'spider', they are asked to write five sentences on a separate sheet of paper, each sentence incorporating an adverb from a different

'spider'. Children can follow this activity with a comparison of each other's words used to complete the 'spiders'.

Photocopiable: Adverb links
This is an investigative activity in which groups of three children explore the type of action and sentence they associate with a particular adverb. The emphasis is on the collation of their findings and, when looking at their results, the examination of the patterns in their outcomes. The children could cut out the sentences they have produced, collecting those which incorporate the same adverbs together, and paste them down onto one large sheet.

Following up
How do you do that?: Children can devise questions that are answerable using adverbs, such as 'How do you walk into a classroom when you are late?', 'How do you walk past a snarling dog?' They can put these to one another and seek out adverbs to provide answers.

Collecting adverbs: As with many of the types of words looked at in this book, an enriching follow-up activity involves children collecting examples. Invite the children to make a list of new and interesting adverbial words and phrases as they read various texts.

Adverb associations: Children can conduct a survey, setting the 'Adverb links' activity for other children and adults and comparing results. They can look at the field of meanings in which the adverbs feature, and perhaps adapt the activity to use new adverbs.

Sort the adverbs

Some adverbs describe **manner**. They show **how** something happened.
He ran quickly.
Some adverbs describe **place**. They show **where** something happened.
He ran upstairs.
Some adverbs describe **time**. They show **when** something happened.
Later, he ran.

❑ Look at the adverbs in the sentences. After each one, write either **manner**, **time** or **place**.

Adverb describes:

The bird sang **sweetly**.	*manner*
Let's go home **now**.	
Come **here**.	
Yesterday there was no school.	
Put the chair **there**.	
He ate **greedily**.	
I will write **soon**.	
We looked **everywhere** for new shoes.	
Tiptoe **quietly** past the guard dog.	
Stop that **immediately**!	
Tuck your shirt **in**.	
We cycled **quickly**.	
He pulled **out** a plum.	
It rained **miserably**.	
The pirate buried the treasure **underground**.	
We **sadly** said 'Goodbye' to our friend.	
I am going swimming **today**.	
Mum carried the baby **upstairs**.	
Shout **loudly** so I can hear.	

Adverb families

❏ Think of four different adverbs to describe each way of doing something. Fill in the 'spiders'.

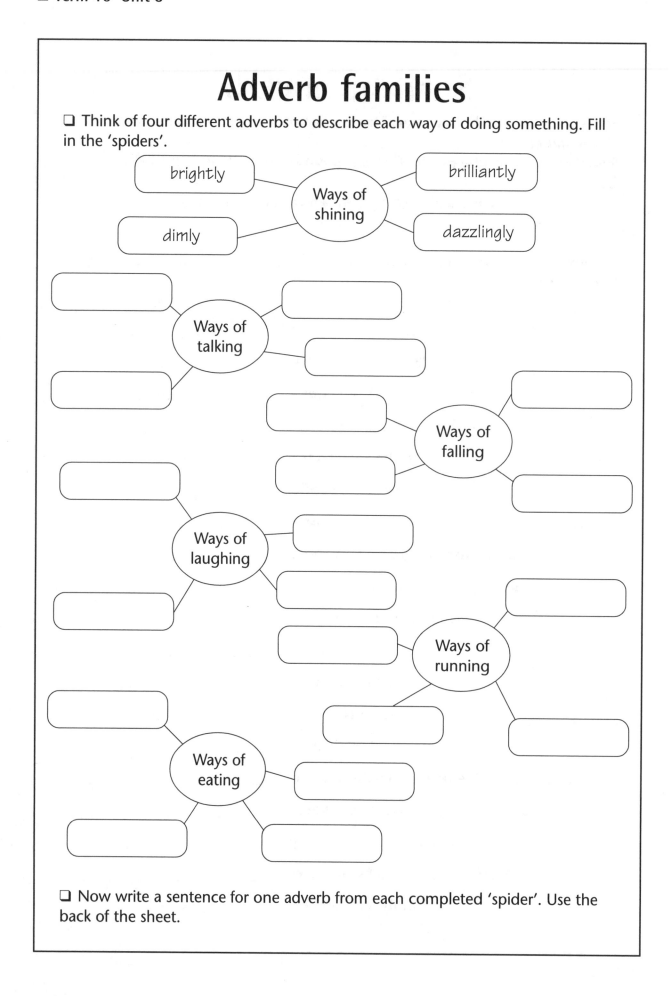

brightly

brilliantly

Ways of shining

dimly

dazzlingly

Ways of talking

Ways of falling

Ways of laughing

Ways of running

Ways of eating

❏ Now write a sentence for one adverb from each completed 'spider'. Use the back of the sheet.

Adverb links

❏ There are eight different adverbs in the boxes below. Write **eight** sentences on a separate sheet of paper, using these adverbs. Use a different adverb in each one. Don't look at anyone else's in your group!

❏ Compare your sentences. Do you notice any similarities? Write what you found out.

Adverb	What we found out
loudly	
greedily	
quietly	
suddenly	
carefully	
sadly	
foolishly	
fearfully	

Changing adverbs

Objective
Investigate the effects of substituting adverbs in particular contexts

Language issues
Selection is an important part of the way we use language. There are a vast number of possible adverbs from which the speaker or writer selects the one to use. Part of the scope for selection of adverbs lies in the fact that most sentences could get by perfectly well without them. Adverbs add information about the verb. Sometimes this is essential. On the other hand, as mentioned in the previous unit, adverbs can be overused, particularly certain adverbs of degree such as 'really' (as in 'I'll tell you what I want, what I really, really want') and 'very'. If something was silly does it make much difference to say it was 'very silly'? or 'very, very silly'? (Teachers take note.)

For this reason it is interesting to look at the selection of adverbs and the way in which apposite words are chosen for the right context.

Ways of teaching
There are no right answers in this unit. Each of the activities offers children the possibility of a range of answers. It is therefore important that you make time for reflection, analysis and more than one 'conclusion'. Through looking at various types of text, children focus on the context as a way into understanding and selecting adverbs.

About the activities
Photocopiable: Suggested adverbs
The two stages to this activity involve, firstly, children devising adverbs to be used in the sentences and secondly, comparing their results. This should demonstrate the idea that we can select and alter a selection of adverbs for a particular sentence. It also provides an opportunity for children to experience having a selection of possible words to fit into a sentence and choosing the best one.

Photocopiable: Possible adverbs
In filling in the word spaces in this activity, children will need to look at the context and the type of adverb most appropriate to it. Again there may be varied results worth comparing. Look out for interesting combinations. This is the sort of activity that shows that, when encouraged, children can be far more daring with language than adults. Children are encouraged to suggest three possibilities for each space. Can they suggest more?

Photocopiable: Adverbs in action
This activity looks at a short extract from a story by Shirley Hughes. The children should have some idea of the context before they read it. It is taken from an early point in the story which is full of suspense. Prior to seeing the girl's face at the window of the gloomy house in which nobody ever comes or goes (except for a big black cat), they have heard 'ghostly screams'.

It is important to stress that suggesting alternative adverbs does not involve improving the text. It is merely to appreciate the way that descriptions of actions can be enhanced by a variety of adverbs, all of equal merit but different in their effect.

Following up
Adverb strings: The children can look at the addition of adverb to adverb to make a string of words modifying the verb. For example, 'Slowly, calmly and steadily, the tightrope walker set off' uses a string of adverbs to describe an action occurring. Children may be able to make similar strings by applying questions such as 'How did it happen? When did it happen? Where did it happen?' to a verb.

Suggested adverbs

❑ Read the following sentences and suggest an adverb that could be inserted in each one. Write them on the lines.

The slug slithered_____up the window.

A star shone_____in the sky.

The car chugged_____to a halt.

The coach shouted_____at the footballers.

_____, a firework shot into the sky.

The bus was leaving so I ran_____.

The children played_____in the playground.

The ball bounced_____and went over the fence.

When they are angry teachers talk_____.

❑ List **five** adverbs you used in some of the sentences.
❑ For each word, find a different adverb you could have put in its place.
❑ Find a different adverb someone else in your class used.
❑ Circle the adverb that you think works best.

Adverb	My alternative adverb	A friend's alternative adverb
1		
2		
3		
4		
5		

Possible adverbs

❑ Read the sentences and write **three** adverbs that could fit in the spaces. You can use adverbs from the word lists. Try using each adverb once.

The dog slept [_____] in his basket, snoozing and snoring. The burglar

moved [_____] up the creaking stairs. But [_____] the dog

woke up. The dog barked [_____] at the burglar. The dog [_____]

chased the burglar. The burglar climbed [_____] up the tree. The dog

growled [_____] at the bottom of the tree. The burglar edged

[_____] along the branch, trying to reach over the wall.

[_____] it snapped.

peacefully	carefully	loudly	hastily	anxiously
dreamily	annoyingly	fiercely	speedily	viciously
pleasantly	suddenly	madly	doggedly	nastily
sneakily	immediately	quickly	hurriedly	cautiously
quietly	gently	fearfully	keenly	slowly

Adverbs in action

❑ Look at this passage from Shirley Hughes's book *It's Too Frightening For Me!*

Jim and Arthur live near an eerie house. The previous day, they have seen a strange girl's face looking out from a window.

Next day they watched from the wall for a long time, but no face appeared. Then Jim noticed a basement door at the bottom of a flight of steps, where the shutter had slipped and a glass pane was broken.

Jim slithered down into the yard and tried the door. It opened! Putting his finger to his lips, Jim made signs to Arthur to stay where he was. Then he disappeared into the house.

Poor Arthur! He badly wanted to run home, but he couldn't desert his brother. After a long while, he too climbed softly down into the yard and, trembling all over, crept in through the basement door to look for Jim.

❑ Some verbs are in the first column. Find them in the story, then find their adverbs (words that say something about the verb). Think of some different adverbs you could use instead of the ones used in the story.

Verbs	Adverbs in the story	Adverbs that could have been used
watched		
slithered		
stay		
wanted		
run		
climbed		
crept		

Commas and sentences

Objective

Practise the use of commas, separating grammatical boundaries within sentences

Language issues

A sentence can consist of one or more clauses. A clause is a group of words linked to a particular verb. It can include a verb and a subject and look like a sentence in itself. So in the sentence 'I like coffee, you like tea' there are two clauses. 'I' is the subject of the verb 'like' in one of the clauses; 'you and 'like' make up the verb and subject of the other. Commas can mark the boundaries between clauses. This can be seen in the 'coffee' and 'tea' sentence.

Commas can also demarcate relative clauses. These are clauses that slot into a sentence giving extra information about things already mentioned. A sentence could state 'Mr Carter mended our cooker'. A clause could be inserted to clarify that Mr Carter lives next door.

This is additional information to develop meaning and the sentence would function without it. The inserted clause is marked off by commas: 'Mr Carter, who lives next door, mended our cooker.'

Ways of teaching

As children develop more complex sentence structures in their writing they can use commas to demarcate clauses. Once they can see the potential for a space in between two commas (or before or after a single comma) into which they can place information, they will find the structure of a sentence much easier to understand and a more complex sentence easier to write; indeed, as we saw with the sentence about Mr Carter above, the complexity can clarify matters when looking at the construction of a sentence and its overall meaning.

About the activities

Photocopiable: Slot into a sentence

This activity gives children the opportunity to practise the insertion of clauses into sentences. It can be used as a springboard to the writing of their own sentences using a similar form.

Ask the children to look at each sentence and see if they can spot where the extra information provided in the clause can be placed. It is important that they read their new sentences as they construct them to check that they make sense. Mention that it may be necessary for them to try saying the sentence with the clause positioned in different places until it works.

Photocopiable: Clauses

This activity involves a process of elimination. The children can look at each sentence to make sure that one of the commas is in the right place. They can then say the sentences out loud reading only the comma they've selected, to help them to decide which commas to remove.

Photocopiable: Dead worried

Place the children into groups for this activity, preferably groups of four or six. (It is useful if they can be evenly numbered.) Ask the children to work in pairs, using a coloured pencil or a felt-tipped pen to insert the commas into the passage. They can then compare their completed sheets with another pair's (copying their commas onto the other pair's sheet using a different colour). At this point they can discuss any differences of opinion. Round off the activity by telling the group where the commas are placed in the original text.

> ### Calm down, Mr King
> Mr King is my school teacher. He's OK, even if he gets a bit worked up some days. Today is one of those days. Behind his steaming glasses, his eyes are glazed with emotion.
>
> "So, Year 6, if we are going to produce some good creative writing for you to take home to your suffering parents, we've got to have creative input. Do you know what input means, Corky?"
>
> Corky, my best mate, blinks and says, "Input. Like output but different. Yes. Sure. Input. Let me think. Um. Putting something in. Yeah."
>
> Mr King glares at him. "That was a lucky guess, Corky." He removes his glasses, wipes them, blots the damp patch on his forehead and breathes heavily.

Following up

Taking sentences apart: Provide the children with other texts which they can look at closely to see where commas have been used to demarcate grammatical boundaries. When they have identified the separate parts of a sentence, they should focus on the question 'What distinctive thing does each part say?'

Rewriting sentences: Reviewing some recent pieces of their writing, children can look at some of the sentences they have used to see if they could have given more information. Could they have put in a relative clause to identify or explain something more clearly?

Slot into a sentence

Each of these sentences has a slip of information between two commas. The slip can be inserted somewhere in the sentence.

❑ Cut out the sentence strip and the slip.

| The big bull escaped and ran through the village. | | , the fiercest on the farm , |

❑ Mark the sentence at the point where you think the slip belongs.
Read the whole sentence.

| The big bull | , the fiercest on the farm, | escaped and ran through the village. |

Does it read well? Does it sound right?
Cut the sentence strip in two at the right point, place the slip in the space in between and stick the new longer sentence onto a sheet of paper.

❑ Now do the same with these sentences and slips.

| Laura starts Nursery today. | , my sister,

| My friend is a great swimmer. | , called Sam Watson,

| My brother dressed smartly today. | , who is usually a scruff,

| For my birthday I want a party. | , in March,

| Our poplar tree blew over in the storm. | , the one on the school field,

| Ms Shell repaired our light switch. | , our school caretaker,

| I might join the school chess team. | , if I get a chance,

| When she gets home my mum has a sleep. | , worn out and tired,

Clauses

He reached out a hand catching the ball.
As it was raining playtime was abandoned.
There is football practice on Tuesday I think.

These can sound odd when you read them.

In each of these sentences one thing is said and then another. There are two chunks. Each of the chunks contains a verb. These chunks are called clauses. A comma separates one clause from another clause.

He reached out a hand, catching the ball.
As it was raining, playtime was abandoned.
There is football practice on Tuesday, I think.

Readers are supposed to pause at the comma.

❑ Look at these sentences. Each contains three commas but only needs **one**. Rewrite the sentences, leaving out two of the commas. Remember to check your sentence by reading it aloud.

She, swung the bat, hitting, the ball.

_____

You want, your coat, I, suppose.

_____

Nassim, walked, slowly, missing the bus.

_____

The plug came out, of the computer, losing, all our work.

_____

The dog, barked, making, the cat jump.

_____

Dead worried

❑ Replace **thirteen** missing commas (remember the title!).

Calm down Mr King

Mr King is my school teacher. He's OK even if he gets a bit worked up some days. Today is one of those days. Behind his steaming glasses his eyes are glazed with emotion.

"So Year 6 if we are going to produce some good creative writing for you to take home to your suffering parents we've got to have creative input. Do you know what input means Corky?"

Corky my best mate blinks and says "Input. Like output but different. Yes. Sure. Input. Let me think. Um. Putting something in. Yeah."

Mr King glares at him. "That was a lucky guess Corky." He removes his glasses wipes them blots the damp patch on his forehead and breathes heavily.

from Dead Worried *by Moya Simons*

Adjectives

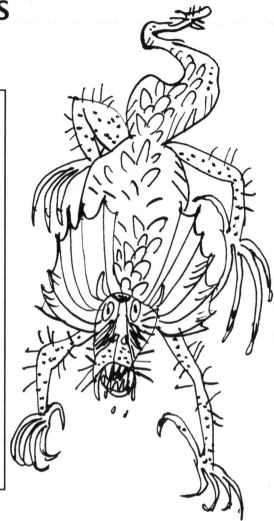

Contents of Term 2a

Unit 1: Revise and extend understanding of
Adjectives adjectives

Unit 2: Understand the use of adjectives in
Similies figurative language

Unit 3: Learn the degrees of intensity that
Intensity adjectives can denote

Unit 4: Understand and use comparative and
Comparative and superlative adjectives
superlative

Unit 5: Investigate the expressive use of adjectives
Expressive adjectives

This half-term

In this half-term the revision of the concept of adjectives is extended into looking at degrees of intensity and expression. The section on similes also develops children's awareness and appreciation of some key adjectival phrases. Terminology such as 'comparative' and 'superlative' provides ways of describing and classifying adjectives. It is also a means of extending children's awareness of the range of adjectives they know, the ones that are available to them and the functions they can perform.

Poster notes

Adjective heap
This is an extended poster version of the adjectives used in 'Choose your adjective' on photocopiable page 60 and provides a resource for activities in which children have to find adjectives to describe things. The examples give children further help in understanding the idea of adjectives.

Jabberwocky
As they look at the poem, children can pick out the words they think are functioning as adjectives. Examples include 'brillig' and 'mimsy'. Once they have listed the 'adjectives', they can try imagining what sort of qualities each one might be describing.

Adjective heap

Jabberwocky

'Twas brillig, and the slithy toves
    Did gyre and gimble in the wabe:
All mimsy were the borogoves,
    And the mome raths outgrabe.

"Beware the Jabberwock, my son!
    The jaws that bite, the claws that catch!
Beware the Jubjub bird, and shun
    The frumious Bandersnatch!"

He took his vorpal sword in hand:
    Long time the manxome foe he sought –
So rested he by the Tumtum tree,
    And stood awhile in thought.

And, as in uffish thought he stood,
    The Jabberwock, with eyes of flame,
Came whiffling through the tulgey wood,
    And burbled as it came!

One, two! One, two! And through and through
    The vorpal blade went snicker-snack!
He left it dead, and with its head
    He went galumphing back.

"And hast thou slain the Jabberwock?
    Come to my arms, my beamish boy!
O frabjous day! Callooh! Callay!"
    He chortled in his joy.

'Twas brillig, and the slithy toves
    Did gyre and gimble in the wabe:
All mimsy were the borogoves,
    And the mome raths outgrabe.

by Lewis Carroll

Adjectives

Objective
Revise and extend understanding of adjectives

Language issues

...word that describes or modifies a noun. ...ngs, it can describe the shape, size or ...noun.

...o be described by adjectival phrases. These ...words that describe a noun.

a perfectly square box
The box is bigger than the ball.
a box as scruffy as me

In each noun phrase there is a headword, an adjective around which the other words are organized.

Ways of teaching
This section should involve revision of introductory work on adjectives in Year 3 (see the Ages 7–8 book in the *Scholastic Literacy Skills: Grammar and Punctuation* series). The activities are extended to include the use of adjectival phrases. As children set about the task of observing adjectives in a variety of contexts, they need to focus on looking for the descriptive word or words and the thing that is being described. In some cases the noun is implicit, as when the blurb on the back cover of a book reads 'brilliant from start to finish'. It is actually referring to 'the book' but the noun is, in such cases, not included.

About the activities
Photocopiable: Choose your adjective
As a way of revising the use of adjectives, this activity asks the children to link adjectives to nouns. They can experiment with various combinations, producing unusual and interesting results in some cases. It is also useful to look at which combinations strike them as unacceptable (and why). How many of the adjectives sit comfortably before the nouns? Which ones don't? Encourage the children to share their findings.

Photocopiable: Adjectival phrases
The task in this activity is to isolate the string of words that is acting as an adjectival phrase and, within it, the headword adjective. Explain that the question 'What is being described?' underpins the process of finding the adjectival phrase.

Photocopiable: Back cover quotes
Book covers often include enthusiastic, adjective-rich endorsements of the product. These examples should act as a starter before the children look at other books to study the adjectival descriptions in the reviews. They could try writing similar quotes for books they know.

Following up
An adjective beginning with…: To play this game, children will need ten cards with ten different letters written on them. Shuffle the cards and place them in a pile, face down. Then ask them to 'Think of an adjective that describes…', inserting a noun. It could be a place, a famous person, a television programme, an event in school – whichever nouns provide an appropriate resource for the game. Having said this, add 'beginning with' and turn over the first card to show its letter. The children then have to come up with an adjective as quickly as they can.

Why those quotes?: The children can collect examples of blurbs on the back covers of books and compare them, asking each other why those particular quotes were used. Why not have one that is less than complimentary? Are the quotes repetitive? How do they affect the reader?

Making blurbs: Provide the children with a current review of a particular children's book, taken from a newspaper or a magazine. Ask them to pinpoint the snippet of text they would print on the back of the book if they were marketing it. Give them a limit of how many words they are allowed for each short piece of text. Alternatively, they could agree on an optimum number themselves by referring to a copy of the photocopiable 'Back cover quotes' on page 62.

Choose your adjective

Here's a pile of adjectives

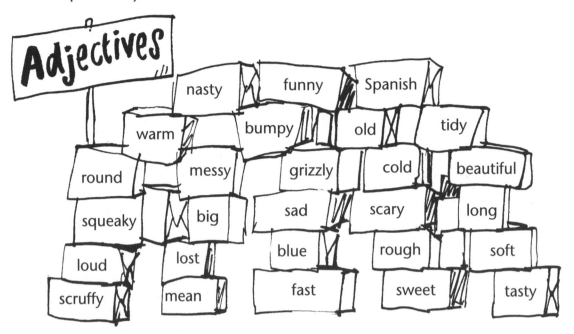

and here's a pile of nouns.

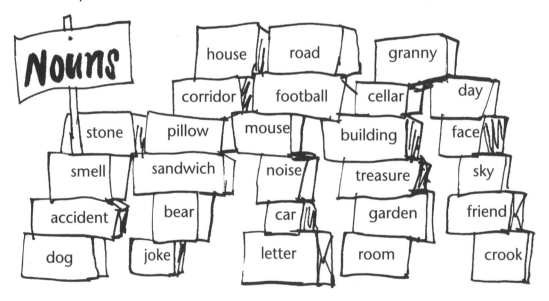

❏ Combine 20 of the nouns with suitable adjectives. Write them down on a separate sheet of paper.

eg ⟨ loud   granny ⟩

Adjectival phrases

An adjectival phrase is a string of words that describes a noun.

| *School is* | *totally brilliant.* |

Adjectival phrases stand in place of single adjectives.

| *School is brilliant.* |

Adjectival phrases contain an adjective.

| *School is* | *totally brilliant.* |

❑ Look at the text in the speech bubbles. In each one find the string of words that is describing the noun. Underline the string of words. Circle the noun being described.

This picnic is more than enough.

My brother has grown to be bigger than me.

She gave me the sweetest, loveliest, dreamiest smile.

The long and winding road leads to the house.

The letter must be lost in the post.

The weather today is hotter than July.

Nothing beats sailing the big, bright, blue sea.

This football is flat as a pancake.

Back cover quotes

❑ Often the back of a book quotes what reviewers said about it. Look through these examples to find adjectives or adjectival phrases. Circle the ones you find.

'Terry Jones is undoubtedly one of the most consistently entertaining writers for children.'
Books for your Children

'Fantasy, adventure and morality are perfectly mixed in this funny, fast-moving story. A marvellous book.'
The Good Book Guide to Children's Books

NICOBOBINUS
BY TERRY JONES

'A truly delightful story… warmly recommended.'
School Librarian

'A lovely book – funny, imaginative and both clever and comforting.'
The Sunday Telegraph

HARVEY ANGELL
BY DIANA HENDRY

'A hugely entertaining novel.'
The Sunday Telegraph

'Anthony Horowitz has created a scary and unmissable old hag.'
The Sunday Times

GRANNY
BY ANTHONY HOROWITZ

'…one of the best books I've ever read. It's funny, moving and it handles difficult subjects with skill and great respect.'
Paula Danziger

'A marvellous book – funny and wise.'
Books for Keeps

TWO WEEKS WITH THE QUEEN
BY MORRIS GLEITZMANN

Similes

Objective
Understand the use of adjectives in figurative language

Language issues
There are a number of ways in which the English language provides users with material for finding figurative ways of saying something. The simile involves the direct linkage of one thing with another thing. The link lies in the similarity between the two. These figurative uses can eventually become fossilized into the language, so although a coot isn't actually bald the expression 'bald as a coot' has such a currency that people ignore the actual appearance of the bird's head.

Similes differ from metaphors. In a metaphor there is also the likening of one thing to another thing, such as the description of a noisy classroom in terms normally associated with a zoo. However, in similes the direct relation is indicated by the words 'as' or 'like', so something is 'dry like the desert' or 'thick as a brick'.

Ways of teaching
Similes can provide children with a clear introduction to the use of figurative language. They can discern the connection between what is being described and what it is being likened to, that is, the term used. In the first two activities in this unit it is this connection that is the focus. The third activity encourages linguistic investigation, looking at some descriptive terms that need studying to seek out their origins.

An essential element of the work in this unit will involve asking children to look out for similes being used in everyday language (see 'Following up').

About the activities
Photocopiable: Match the simile
Make an enlarged copy of the sheet for the initial stage of this activity. After you have introduced the idea of similes, point out the gap in the first sentence. The children need to ask themselves: 'Which adjective can link the two parts of the sentence?' Explain that this linking is how similes extend the description of something. Go through the next sentence, finding its missing simile as a class, before the children complete the sheet individually or in groups.

Photocopiable: Descriptive similes
This activity builds on the previous one by asking the children to devise some examples of similes of their own, one for each of their chosen subjects.

Photocopiable: Old similes
Encourage the children to read closely the information given for each noun. Then they will be able to work out the correct words to complete the similes – that is, the adjectives with which the nouns are associated. The answers are:

wise as Solomon	thin as a lath
cool as a cucumber	rich as Croesus
dead as a dodo	mad as a March hare
bald as a coot	sure as death and taxes
sour as vinegar	plain as a pikestaff
patient as Job	limp as a glove

Following up
Simile collecting: Once they have been introduced to the concept of similes, children will often give examples of ones they hear used by adults around them. This can be extended by asking children to make a list of similes at home. They can interview any adults and try making a list of ten. On returning to school, lists can be compared to find common ones and ones unique to their family.

Literary similes: Ask the children to look out for examples of similes in stories and poems they are reading. Wordsworth wandering lonely as a cloud is one of the best known but there are countless other examples.

Modern similes: The children can look at some of the cultural and historical references in old similes and try to devise their own new ones. Point out that, within a few years, these will also be dated! Which name could they put in place of Croesus in 'as rich as Croesus'? They can use names from the contemporary worlds of business, pop, film and sport.

Match the simile

Similes can be used to describe nouns. They link a description of something to a similar thing.

as slow as a snail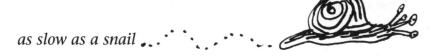

The words **as** and **like** are often used to make a simile.
For example:
You're as daft as a brush.
He's as cool as a cucumber.

❏ Look at these broken similes. Write in the correct words to repair them.

A spring morning is		as a lemon.
The morning went by		as a racing car.
Our teacher was		like a clown.
My brother is		like a giant.
Our baby is		like a kitten.
The secretary is		as a bee.
Your answers were		as a knife.
The classroom was		as a graveyard.
The children were		as a herd of elephants.
The joke fell		as a pancake.

as fast	as noisy	tall	playful	as sharp
cheerful	as quiet	as flat	as fresh	as busy

Descriptive similes

Simile maker
Think of the thing you're describing.
Think of a quality about it or a descriptive word for it.
Think of something that shares this quality.
Link the two together – you could use the words **as** or **like**.

❑ Here are some subjects.
Pick **fifteen** and create a simile for each of them.

My friend

Playtimes

The classroom

Football

Assembly

Cycling   School dinner

The park

English

Grandad

The news

The supermarket

Maths

My favourite
chocolate bar   A bus journey

The weather today

A bully   My bedroom

Home

Snails

School

Salad

Swimming   Waking up

Old similes

❏ Look at these old similes. The missing word in each simile could be any of the nouns listed in the table. To help you match each noun to its simile, a little note is included with each one, explaining its origin.

wise as _____	sour as _____	mad as _____
cool as _____	patient as _____	sure as _____
dead as _____	thin as _____	plain as _____
bald as _____	rich as _____	limp as _____

a coot A coot is a bird whose white bill extends to make a shield over its head.	**Croesus** Croesus was an ancient king said to have great wealth.
vinegar Have you ever drunk a little bit of vinegar? What does it taste like?	**a pikestaff** A pikestaff was a long pole with a spear tip, sometimes measuring 16 feet and very hard to conceal.
Solomon Solomon was a king in the Bible who had the gift of great wisdom.	**a March hare** During the month of March, mating hares exhibit strange, crazy behaviour.
Job In the Bible, Job went through terrible times but remained faithful and thoughtful.	**a lath** A long, slim piece of wood, only about 2 to 3cm wide, used in fences and as a support for slates.
a dodo Dodos were a Portuguese species of bird which became extinct in the late 17th century.	**a glove** How does a glove change when you take your hand out?
death and taxes These are two things many people would rather avoid, but are pretty sure to face.	**a cucumber** On a warm day the centre of a cucumber has a lower temperature than the air around it.

Intensity

Objective
Learn the degrees of intensity that adjectives can denote

Language issues
A sentence involves a combination of words. There is a process of selection involved in the use of the individual words. One of the finer points of this process of selection concerns the intensity of the adjectives.

If someone spills a drop of tea on the tablecloth, they may say, 'Oh, that's annoying,' but they would be exaggerating if they deemed it 'completely disastrous'. Adjectives have links with other adjectives, and some of them are more extreme than others.

Ways of teaching
This unit deals with convention in the use of adjectives, so there will be an element of subjective judgement. Many people will consider the word 'disastrous' to be more extreme than 'irritating' on the scale of describing the unpleasantness of something. However, language changes and, within families or groups of friends, certain terms can take on a currency of their own. When I was at school we had a teacher who used the word 'transmogrified' about a situation. Some of us fell in love with the word and from then on any situation that went awry, whether it was spilling tea or a turn for the worse in the weather, was described as 'transmogrified'.

About the activities
Photocopiable: Ordering adjectives
This activity looks at the way adjectives can be compared with each other when focusing on a particular quality, such as the brightness of a light ('dim', 'bright', 'dazzling', 'blinding'). Children might be able to think of other adjectives that are similar to the ones given in a particular row and slot them in so that they are in their correct positions within the scale (for example, the word 'warm' could be placed in between 'cold' and 'hot' in the first row).

Photocopiable: Adjective links
An essential part of the process of selecting the appropriate adjective in a particular context is the stock of words the speaker or writer has to call upon. This activity encourages children to look at the variety of adjectives that can be linked to a particular context. The easiest way for the children to carry it out is to start with one adjective, link it to a noun and then find other words that can be substituted for their initial adjective.

Photocopiable: Your intensity scale
Returning to the earlier example, there are those for whom a spillage on the tablecloth is a heinous and grave disaster most foul. The intensity of adjectives used to describe something like a spider will vary according to the person making the description. This activity asks children to explore the varying intensity of their responses to different things. They can use their 'Adjective links' completed photocopiable sheet to provide material for it.

Following up
'Hot and Cold': The old game in which people would hide something in a room and, as someone else looked for it, guide them as to how close they were by saying 'Cold… cool… warmer…' can be adapted. The game relied upon variable temperature as a guide to how close the seeker was to the hidden object. The same game can be played using other scales of intensity, such as those used for happiness and sadness, fear and confidence.

Thesauruses: The links activity on photocopiable page 69 can be extended to include the use of thesauruses. Children can be encouraged to find new and unfamiliar adjectives.

Compare the scale: Ask the children to look at their comparisons of intensity on their completed copies of photocopiable page 70, and to write the nouns on one set of cards and the adjectives on another. Can their friends match the cards up? Do they match the adjectives to the nouns in the same way? Let the children record the results, with the aim of finding out if there are particular cards that are always chosen as a matching set, evoking the same response.

Ordering adjectives

❏ Can you sort the adjectives so that the words are in the correct order in each row? Cut them out and place them in order from one extreme to the other.

For example:
The first row contains words which are all about temperature. You could arrange them like this – from hottest to coldest.

| boiling | | | freezing |

a _____ day	cold	boiling	freezing	hot
feeling _____	happy	overjoyed	miserable	sad
a _____ door	closed	open	ajar	wide open
feeling _____	calm	cross	angry	furious
a _____ landscape	flat	rolling	hilly	mountainous
a _____ bike	sluggish	speedy	fast	slow
a _____ person	big	huge	tiny	small
a _____ light	dim	bright	blinding	dazzling

Adjective links

❑ Collect together similar sets of adjectives. Try to get **five** or more adjectives in each set.
For example:

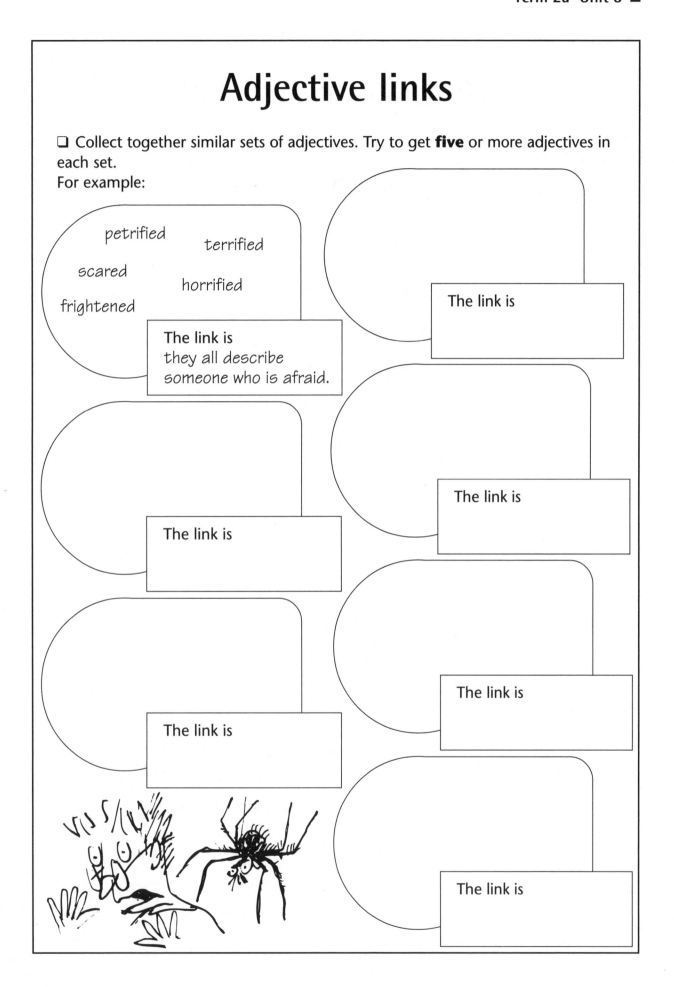

petrified

terrified

scared

horrified

frightened

The link is
they all describe
someone who is afraid.

The link is

The link is

The link is

The link is

The link is

The link is

The link is

Your intensity scale

Each row shows two adjectives. They move from the less intense to the more intense.

❑ Can you think of something you would describe using the two different words?

Noun	Adjective 1	Adjective 2
_____	good	brilliant
_____	warm	hot
_____	tasty	delicious
_____	smooth	slippery
_____	smelly	stinking
_____	simple	easy peasy
_____	scary	terrifying
_____	quiet	silent
_____	cold	freezing

❑ Now see if you can make up your own examples.

Noun	Adjective 1	Adjective 2
_____	_____	_____
_____	_____	_____
_____	_____	_____
_____	_____	_____

Comparative and superlative

Objective
Understand and use comparative and superlative adjectives

Language issues
Adjectives can indicate the degree to which a noun possesses a particular quality. This is done by using three different forms of adjective: the nominative (or the 'positive') is the plain form of the adjective indicating the quality of a noun (for example, 'This tree is tall'); the comparative implies a comparison between a noun and another noun or nouns (for example, 'This tree is taller'); the superlative is an adjective indicating that its noun is the extreme example of a particular quality (for example, 'This tree is tallest').

There are various ways of making the nominative form comparative and superlative.

❑ In many cases adding 'er' to the nominative makes the comparative:

big ➜ bigger

and adding 'est' to the positive makes the superlative:

big ➜ biggest

❑ For adjectives ending in 'y', the 'y' is changed to 'i' before the additions are made.

pretty ➜ prettier ➜ prettiest

❑ Longer adjectives tend to use the words 'more' and 'most' to make the comparative and superlative:

beautiful ➜ more beautiful ➜ most beautiful

rather than

beautiful ➜ beautifuller ➜ beautifullest

❑ There are some exceptions to both these rules, for example:

good ➜ better ➜ best

bad ➜ worse ➜ worst

Ways of teaching
Children like latching on to big words. The terminology used in this unit is appealing to children because even though it is fairly easy to find, identify and create examples of the three types of adjective, they have these marvellous terms – nominative, comparative, superlative – attached to them! Children can learn the trio of terms almost like a rhyme.

bad

worse

worst

About the activities
Photocopiable: Nominative, comparative, superlative
This activity asks the children to sort the adjectives into the three varying degrees (linking to the photocopiable 'Ordering adjectives' in the previous unit, which introduces children to the idea of sorting adjectives in a general way).

Photocopiable: Varieties of comparison
In order to grasp the various ways in which the adjectives can be made, one rule for deciding whether to alter the endings or use 'more' or 'most' is to count the syllables: one-syllable adjectives tend to use 'er' and 'est'; two syllable adjectives can do either; three-syllable adjectives tend to use 'more' and 'most'.

Photocopiable: Ordering by degree
As a reinforcement activity, this task involves children in devising trios of nouns to fit trios of adjectives.

Following up
Characters: Ask the children to think of adjectives that can be used to describe personalities (for example, 'nasty', 'happy') and to make a comparative trio for each adjective ('nasty', 'nastier', 'nastiest' and so on). Do they know any characters in stories they have read that could fit each adjective in the trio?

Bidding: Ask a group of children to think of something that can be described by using a particular adjective. For example, a cartoon could be 'silly'. Explain that they then have to think of comparative examples. Working with the adjective 'miserable', for example, they may decide that a cold day is 'miserable' and that playtime on a cold day is 'more miserable'. As the activity progresses, they can record their examples until they have a scale of progress concerning the adjective they are using, with an example for the superlative form at the end (which for 'most miserable' could be playtime on a cold, drizzly, winter's day when the football has been confiscated!).

Records: Books like *The Guinness Book of Records* can be referred to for examples of recognized superlatives. Children can think of an adjective and use their referencing skills to see if there are any records for the adjective in its superlative form (for example, 'tallest' may present a range of examples including mountains, people, buildings, trees and so on).

Nominative, comparative, superlative

An adjective can have three degrees.

There is the plain adjective, sometimes called the **nominative**,

the adjective that compares, the **comparative**

and the adjective that beats them all, the **superlative**.

I am short.

I am shorter.

I am shortest.

❑ Write out these adjectives, sorting them into order – nominative, comparative and superlative.

| tallest | tall | taller |

| smarter | smart | smartest |

| happiest | happier | happy |

| cool | coolest | cooler |

| juicy | juicier | juiciest |

| thin | thinnest | thinner |

| hotter | hot | hottest |

| unhappiest | unhappy | unhappier |

Varieties of comparison

The three degrees of adjective can be made by altering the ending of the word:

quiet	*quiet**er***	*quiet**est***
silly	*sill**ier***	*sill**iest***

> When you make the changes with adjectives ending in **y** you change **y** to **i**.

They can also be made with the words **more** and **most**:

quiet	***more** quiet*	***most** quiet*
silly	***more** silly*	***most** silly*

There are also trios that don't fit any rule.

good	*better*	*best*
bad	*worse*	*worst*

❑ Try the different ways of making the three degrees with these adjectives. Check by seeing if the trio sounds right when you say it.

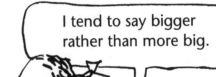

> Beautiful… beautifuller… beautifullest – doesn't sound right.

> I tend to say bigger rather than more big.

Nominative	Comparative	Superlative
long		
honest		
small		
dangerous		
young		
old		
different		
sharp		
peaceful		
careful		
brilliant		
tall		

Ordering by degree

❑ Fill in the boxes with trios of nouns that fit the adjectives.
For example:

A spider	is scary	A poisonous spider	is scarier	A kid-eating, poisonous spider	is scariest
	is scary		is scarier		is scariest
	is good		is better		is best
	is fast		is faster		is fastest
	is big		is bigger		is biggest
	is dangerous		is more dangerous		is most dangerous
	is tasty		is tastier		is tastiest

Expressive adjectives

Objective
Investigate the expressive use of adjectives

Language issues
The poetic quality of adjectives can be seen in a wide range of texts. From pop songs ('A Hard Day's Night') and poetry ('It is spring, moonless night…') to sports reporting (see photocopiable page 77), adjectives can be used in ways that evoke images and enrich the way something is denoted.

Ways of teaching
This unit provides ways of exploring this diverse and poetic use of adjectives. A variety of source material is drawn upon including common speech, rap poetry and a football report. What is essential is that these are used as a springboard to a fuller exploration of the use of adjectives. Once children have encountered them in these texts they will hopefully look for them elsewhere.

About the activities
Photocopiable: How you say it
This activity asks children to list a range of adjectives encountered in everyday speech that can be used to describe some of the high and low feelings in life. Descriptions of this nature attract a vast range of expressions, both in standard English and non-standard English. In South Wales, for example, a person who is ill can be ill in three varying degrees: 'bad' or 'bad in bed' or even 'bad in bed and under the doctor'!

Children might want to keep a note of the names of the people whom they have heard use the expressions. They can also ask adults at home to try to remember some expressions from their own youth. There may be some teachers who are able to furnish them with a repertoire that includes 'fab' and 'ace'.

Photocopiable: Match report
For this activity, the children will need access to a range of newspapers. It will have an obvious relevance if reports of a recent and important game can be circulated.

Photocopiable: Boasts
As children read the boasts and try to write their own, they will need to consider the most extreme ways in which the quality they have chosen could manifest itself. They may even want to perform an enactment of their boasts as a drama activity.

Following up
Adjective collage: The whole class can contribute to a collection of sentences cut out from adverts, articles, leaflets, letters and so on, collecting together interesting uses of adjectives. Stress that the collection should omit adjectives that could be considered to be 'plain' or 'normal'; only those that are interesting or different in some way should be included. Sentences from various texts can be cut out and added to a large sheet of paper.

Streetwise adjectives: The search for varied adjectives can spill into the playground and other places where children talk among themselves. They can analyse some of the words they use for describing things. There are often various ways of saying something is good ('wicked', 'cool') or easy ('easy, peasy, lemon squeezy'), for example.

Adjectival characters: Adjectives can often provide names for characters, for example Superman, the Incredible Hulk, Scary Spice, Desperate Dan. Provide the children with some comics or magazines which they can hunt through to list the adjectival names used. Can they recall characters from television programmes who have adjectives in their names? Ask them to think of five new adjectives to use as starting points for the creation of new characters.

How you say it

Benjamin Zephaniah's poem starts with four positive descriptions of 'dat guy'.

▶ Dat guy **BAD**
He's ***kicking***,
He's *wicked*,
C R U C I A L

❑ People use different adjectives for different things. Ask various people what adjectives they use to describe people. List their responses.

good	**nasty**
He or she is	He or she is

tired	**ill**
He or she is	He or she is

sad	**crazy**
He or she is	He or she is

Match report

Football reports use some incredible adjectives. Look at this extract and find some examples.

Christian Vieri… is a striker who has blasted into this World Cup with a ready supply of goals in his boots. A solitary deadly strike, his fifth of the tournament, shot Italy into the quarter finals. Once the deed was done the reliable, impenetrable defence clicked the lock shut… It was the mighty attacking presence of Vieri who looked the most dangerous force on the field.

© *The Observer (28 June 1998)*

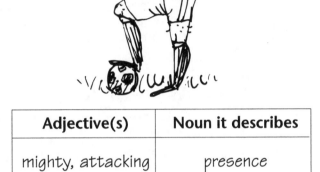

Adjective(s)	Noun it describes
mighty, attacking	presence

❑ Collect two more extracts from a newspaper that give some good examples of adjectives and list some of the adjectives used. You could use a football report, too, if you like.

Adjective(s)	Noun

Boasts

Here are some boasts collected from various people and places:

I know someone who
can run so fast
he meets himself
coming back.

I know someone who's
so good at jumping
she can jump across a
river and back without
touching the other
side.

There's a man round here
who is so tall
he has to climb a ladder to shave himself
when he was born he was so big
it was impossible to name all of him at once
he grew so fast
his head grew three inches through the top of his hat.

Adapted from a collection in The Kingfisher book of Children's Poetry
selected by Michael Rosen.

Each one boasts about an adjective:

so fast   so tall
        so good at jumping   so big

❑ Try making up your own incredible boasts. Start with:

I know someone who is so...

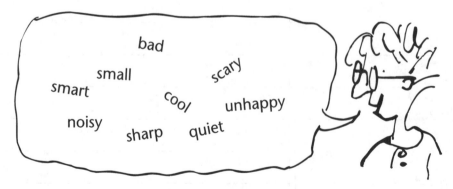

bad
small   scary
smart   cool   unhappy
noisy   sharp   quiet

Apostrophes, word order, connectives

Contents of Term 2b

Unit 1:
Apostrophes for possession
Identify possessive apostrophes in reading and writing and to whom or what they refer

Unit 2:
Apostrophes for contraction
Distinguish between apostrophe for possession and contraction

Unit 3:
Apostrophes in use
Understand the uses of the apostrophe in reading and writing

Unit 4:
Word order
Investigate the significance of word order

Unit 5:
Connectives
Understand the way in which clauses are connected

This half-term

Each of the units in this half-term show how language can be refined to provide clarity of expression. The apostrophe can indicate possession where it would otherwise be ambiguous. Word order can prove important in clarifying exactly what a sentence is saying.

Poster notes

Apostrophe chart
This supports Unit 1 by providing a poster version of the rules for the addition of apostrophes to show possession. As a class, collect further examples of the four different categories of the possessive apostrophe and display them on a large sheet next to the poster. Can the children spot all the nouns that are objects of possession? Can they provide further examples?

Connectives
This poster presents the main functions of connecting words. It underpins the work in Unit 5 as children are asked not just to identify the ways in which clauses are connected but also to understand the functions of the various connectives.

Apostrophe chart

This chart shows the rules for adding an apostrophe of possession.

	Noun is singular	**Noun is plural**
Noun doesn't end in 's'	Add apostrophe and 's' eg *Sam* in *Sam's dog* Add apostrophe and 's'	Add apostrophe and 's' eg *children* in *children's dog*
Noun ends in 's'	Add apostrophe and 's' eg *Paris* in *Paris's tower*	Add apostrophe eg *babies* in *babies' rattles*

Connectives

Type of connection	Function	Examples
Addition	words to add things	and also I like my school and I like my classroom.
Opposition	words to oppose things	but however I went out to play but I felt ill.
Cause	things causing other things	because so therefore The match was called off because it was raining.
Time	the times when things happened	then and then after I went to the shop then I called for my friend.

Apostrophes for possession

Objective
Identify possessive apostrophes in reading and writing and to whom or what they refer

Language issues
Apostrophes can be used to show possession. An apostrophe in a word that is a noun can show it possesses a following item, for example 'Sean's book'. Rules for adding apostrophes depend on the nouns to which they are being added.

If the noun is singular and doesn't end in 's', you add an apostrophe and an 's', for example:
Sam's dog
Kate's football

If the noun is singular and ends in 's', you add an apostrophe and an 's', for example:
Ross's cat
Paris's tower

If the noun is plural and doesn't end in 's', you add an apostrophe and an 's', for example:
the children's dog
the mice's nest

If the noun is plural and ends in 's', you add an apostrophe but don't add an 's', for example:
the babies' rattles
the teachers' mugs

Ways of teaching
When learning punctuation rules like these, the most effective introduction is for children to have access to the rules and to try them out on a variety of words and phrases. The activities in this unit ask children to look at various examples of the different rules.

About the activities
Photocopiable: Reading apostrophes
As an introductory example, children are asked to read some sentences and examine the relationship between the word that contains the apostrophe and the word which is the object of posession.

Photocopiable: Our lists
This activity involves children in the task of making lists of phrases that include apostrophes.

Photocopiable: Singular and plural
In this activity children encounter the various rules for adding apostrophes of possession to nouns. They then try a set of examples. The two crucial questions about the noun are 'Is it singular or plural?' and 'Does it end in the letter "s"?' (see the poster on photocopiable page 80).

Following up
Examples: Provide the children with reading material in which they can find examples of the possessive apostrophe that cover each of the rules. Can they think of their own examples of phrases that use apostrophes for possession? Suggest that they compile examples which are inspired by characters from books or television.

Examining examples: When children find examples of apostrophes used to indicate possession in their reading, encourage them to use the 'Reading apostrophes' photocopiable sheet on page 83 to examine the relationship between the word with the apostrophe and the noun to which it belongs.

Reading apostrophes

❑ Look at these sentences. In each there is a word with a possessive apostrophe. Something belongs to the noun that ends with the apostrophe.

Look at Sam's dog.

The apostrophe shows:
The dog belongs to Sam.

❑ Complete the sentences, showing who or what 'possesses' something.

Sophie's bike is really fast.

The _____ belongs to _____ .

Mr Hall repaired the guitar's string.

The _____ belongs to _____ .

Maya collected each class's register.

The _____ belongs to _____ .

We found a stripy snail's shell.

The _____ belongs to _____ .

Everyone waited for the orchestra's conductor.

The _____ belongs to _____ .

The farmer put the cows' food in their trough.

The _____ belongs to _____ .

After school, Micah and Louie went to Toby's house.

The _____ belongs to _____ .

Our lists

Jamie asked eight children in his class, 'What is your favourite toy?' He recorded the results using apostrophes to show who said what.

Tracy's football
Kirpan's magic set
Caroline's troll
Jan's train set
Harry's space rider
Tara's chemistry set
Kyle's yo-yo
Nathan's computer game

❏ Ask children in your class each question and make a list under each heading. Remember to use the apostrophe.

Best toy	Clothing	Relative who gets the most visits
Which toy is your absolute favourite?	What's your favourite item of clothing?	Which of your relatives do you visit the most?

Singular and plural

Where you place an apostrophe depends on the word it is added to.

The owner	The rule	Examples
is singular, doesn't end in 's'	add an apostrophe and 's'	*Sam's dog* *Kate's football*
is singular, ends in 's'	add an apostrophe and 's'	*Ross's cat* *Paris's tower*
is plural, doesn't end in 's'	add an apostrophe and 's'	*the children's dog* *the mice's nest*
is plural, ends in 's'	add an apostrophe only (no 's')	*the babies' rattles* *the teachers' mugs*

❏ Look at this sentence.

The bike belongs to Pete.

Turn it into a phrase that
has an apostrophe. It becomes:

Pete's bike

> Look at the thing or person who owns. Is there one or more? Does the word end in 's'?

❏ Turn these sentences into phrases that have apostrophes.

The football belongs to Kate. _____

The quiz game belongs to the class. _____

The playground belongs to the children. _____

The mugs belong to the teachers. _____

The lids belong to the boxes. _____

The houses belong to the people. _____

The farm belongs to the women. _____

The driver belongs to the bus. _____

The cat belongs to Ross. _____

Apostrophes for contraction

Objective
Distinguish between apostrophe for possession and contraction

Language issues
Apostrophes can mark possession but they can also mark the contraction of a word or words. They show where two words have been contracted together with some of the letters removed, marking the point at which the letters once stood, so 'did not', for example, loses the 'o' to become 'didn't'.

In many cases the apostrophe marks a contraction of words that we would not now use. People tend not to say 'I did not…' unless it's for emphasis. We usually say 'I didn't…' In 'o'clock' the apostrophe marks a contraction of a phrase ('of the clock') that has dropped out of common usage.

There is an ongoing development of the apostrophe's use, such that it now features in contractions like 'should've' and 'must've'. These contractions are not favoured in some quarters but it remains to be seen whether they stick around.

Ways of teaching
As children come across an apostrophe they can look to see if it is marking contraction or possession. They then need to ask, if it is an apostrophe of possession, 'What belongs to whom?' If it is an apostrophe of contraction they can try to identify the words that are being contracted, the words that are 'behind' the phrase that is apostrophized.

About the activities
Photocopiable: Contraction
By matching the two sets of words, children are able to look at some of the common contractions and the words they contract.

Photocopiable: Contraction or possession?
This activity asks children to identify examples of apostrophes used for contraction and those used for possession. Each word containing an apostrophe is highlighted so that the children can see at a glance which words they should focus on. As they classify the apostrophes remind them to consider the key points given in 'Ways of teaching'.

Photocopiable: Sort the apostrophes
The story contains 17 apostrophes, eight of possession, nine of contraction. As children find them they can record them using formats they will be familiar with from earlier activities.

Following up
Contraction detecting: Children can tape a conversation and listen for the contractions in their speech when they play it back. Ask them to tape a five-minute discussion about a theme with which they are all familiar and on which they all have opinions. They can then play back the tape as many times as they need to, stopping and noting down any contractions in their speech.

Varied contractions: Ask the children to list any new contractions they encounter in their reading or in their everyday conversations. It is likely that there will be a number of contemporary or localized contractions they will use in speech, such as 'ain't', 'tha's kiddin' '.

Contraction

Apostrophes are used to contract words together. This means that we can write them down in the way we say them.

Instead of saying
Lola ate the cake she had made,
people often say
Lola ate the cake she'd made.

When we write this we use the apostrophe.
It shows where something has been removed.

Lola ate the cake she ↓ *d made.*
        ha

Lola ate the cake she'd made.

❑ Write the contractions alongside the original phrases.

we will _____

he will _____

does not _____

it is _____

he would _____

have not _____

is not _____

cannot _____

let us _____

do not _____

did not _____

you will _____

you are _____

we have _____

she would _____

must not _____

she will _____

I will _____

I am _____

could not _____

couldn't   can't   mustn't

she'd   didn't   you're

doesn't   we'll   let's

she'll   don't

he'd   haven't

I'm

he'll

I'll   isn't

you'll

we've   it's

Contraction or possession?

❑ Look at the sentences. Sort them into two groups. Put a 'P' in the box for a sentence that has an apostrophe of possession. Put a 'C' in the box for a sentence that has an apostrophe of contraction. The words have been circled to help you.

Chris (can't) remember his house in Scotland. ☐

(Chris's) family come from Scotland. ☐

(Don't) put too much food in the fish tank. ☐

(I'll) check that (we've) closed the classroom door. ☐

I think (I'll) go to the park after school. ☐

My class (hasn't) done PE this week. ☐

My grandpa said (he'd) meet me from school. ☐

On (Mum's) birthday we made her a cake. ☐

Some people are painting the (doctor's) surgery. ☐

The cook made the (children's) dinners. ☐

The farmer sheared the (sheep's) wool. ☐

The plug on the hoover (didn't) work. ☐

Sort the apostrophes

❑ Look at this piece of writing and find the apostrophes of possession and the apostrophes of contraction. List them on a separate sheet of paper, and show how they work:

For an apostrophe of possession, write

the _____ of the _____

(for example, *the journey of the sheep*)

For an apostrophe of contraction, write
the full form of the word after the contraction

(for example, *he'd – he would*)

One day a shepherd thought he'd take his sheep to a new, green hillside. The sheep's journey took them down some difficult paths. One little lamb couldn't keep up. The shepherd didn't see a wolf sneak up and grab her. The wolf was about to eat her when the lamb noticed the wolf's whistle in his pocket.

"Oh you mustn't eat me," she said. "I can't die without a send-off."

The wolf was puzzled.

"Please play your whistle," she said. "I'll do a little dance for my funeral and then you'll eat me."

Even more puzzled, the wolf agreed to the lamb's request.

He played and the lamb danced, but the shepherd heard the wolf's music. He sent his fierce dogs. As the shepherd's dog chased him away the wolf realized the lamb's trick.

"That'll teach me a lesson," he said. "I've been tricked into doing a musician's job instead of a wolf's."

Based on a fable by Aesop

Apostrophes in use

Objective
Understand the uses of the apostrophe in reading and writing

Language issues
The apostrophe enjoys a varied usage. It joined the English language from French in the 16th century and its usage spread from contraction to possession. It now gets overused, sometimes being inserted before any '-s' ending (for example, 'pop and crisp's', 'Carpet's at bargain prices'). At the other extreme it has dropped out of usage in many contexts, deemed to be unnecessary as the job it would be doing can often be gauged from the context in which it would be used. This can be seen in product logos and signs. It features on Cadbury's products and in the name Waterstone's, but not on Levis jeans, for example.

Ways of teaching
This unit presents materials in which children look closely at how apostrophes are used. An important way in which children will develop their understanding of this punctuation mark is by undertaking the process of reading texts that contain examples of apostrophes, followed by reviewing where they could have used them in their own writing.

About the activities
Photocopiable: Santa Fe
This complicated poem is made comprehensible by its apostrophes. The children are asked to make sense of the action in the fourth, fifth and sixth stanzas. One way of doing this would be to write the characters' names – Cook, Turkey and Jelly – next to the ones the poet uses. They can then figure out who is eating whom!

Photocopiable: Redrafting
It is crucial that this redrafting activity is not seen as an end in itself. It should act as a starter only, with children getting into the habit of looking at their use of apostrophes when they redraft their work generally.

Photocopiable: Usage survey
Starting with names of restaurants, the children are asked to look at the usage of the apostrophe. This involves them in an aspect of language that is undergoing change, as the apostrophe drifts out of use in a number of contexts. Let the activity lead in to a discussion of the usefulness of the apostrophe.

Following up
Redrafting: Children can review pieces of their own writing, finding points at which they could have used apostrophes.

Uses around us: Ask the children to look out for uses of the apostrophe on shop signs and notices. They may notice examples of the apostrophe misused.

Phone-book doubles: Children can scan the phone book for examples of businesses with identical names, bar the apostrophe. Two businesses called Paulines may be listed, but one may be 'Pauline's' and the other 'Paulines'. They could do some investigative reporting into how companies become listed in the phone book and what checking process there is over punctuation, perhaps speaking to local businesses about their use of the apostrophe in their business names.

The variety of ways in which the apostrophe is used in everyday language offers children a chance to look at the creation and establishment of a convention – rather than just learning the rules that govern its use!

Santa Fe

❏ Look at the poem. Try to work out what is happening. Write notes alongside stanzas 4, 5 and 6.

It was a stormy night
one Christmas day
as they fell awake
on the Santa Fe

Turkey, jelly
and the ship's old cook
all jumped out
of a recipe book

The jelly wobbled
the turkey gobbled
and after them both
the old cook hobbled

Gobbler gobbled
Hobbler's Wobbler.
Hobbler gobbled
Wobbler's Gobbler.

Gobbly-gobbler
gobbled Wobbly
Hobbly-hobbler
Gobbled Gobbly.

Gobbler gobbled
Hobble's Wobble
Hobble gobbled
gobbled Wobble.

gobble gobble
wobble wobble
hobble gobble
wobble gobble

from *Mind Your Own Business* by Michael Rosen

> Three clues:
> the 'Hobbler' is the cook,
> the 'Gobbler' is the turkey,
> the 'Wobbler' is the jelly.

Redrafting

❑ Look at this piece of writing. Check the apostrophes. Are there:
• singular and plural uses of the apostrophe of possession?
• apostrophes of contraction in the right place?
• apostrophes placed only where they are needed?

Yesterday I went to Sams house. I have'nt been there before. Sams brother Chris was there. Hes at college. We played on Chri'ss computer. Hed only had it a week. Then Sam said "Lets' go to the park, so we did.' Our friends were there. We joined in our friends's game, swinging on the playgrounds railings.

   We couldnt' stay because Sams mum called us in for tea.

   Sam was slurping his soup. His mum said, "Thats disgusting. Dont slurp."

   We ate really quickly and Sam said, "Weve got to go out again now."

   "No you dont," his Mum said, "its' time for Paul to go home."

   So we sulked.

❑ Write down your corrected version on a separate sheet of paper.

Usage survey

The apostrophe is sometimes used too much.

Or it is not used when it could have been.

❏ Photocopy a column of restaurants from the Yellow Pages telephone directory. Stick it on the box.

❏ Put a circle around the restaurants that name the owner.

How many could have used an apostrophe but don't?

How many do use an apostrophe?

❏ Look at other sections of the phone book or at local shop signs and try to find examples of 'left-out' apostrophes.

Word order

Objective
Investigate the significance of word order

Language issues
Word order is a key element of the way users of English combine selected words together in sentences. Children develop it in spoken English, moving from early constructions such as 'Dad me give' to the conventional form of word order.

Word order can greatly affect a sentence. It can lead to meaningless sentences ('The on sat mat cat' instead of 'The cat sat on the mat') and it can alter the meaning of sentences (so 'The cat sat on the mat' can become 'The mat sat on the cat').

In English there are a variety of word orders that can be used. The plain form of subject, verb and object is the most common, but variations can be found throughout the usage of the language. The famous ending to the Goldsmith poem about the mad dog that bit the man is an example of an unusual ordering of words that has a resonant effect, and it enables us to see the scope for varied constructions:

The man recovered of the bite,
The dog it was that died.

Ways of teaching
This unit focuses on the alteration of meaning through the changing of word order. Activities look at some of the conventions of word order and games that can be played with them.

About the activities
Photocopiable: Sounds right?
The ending to the Goldsmith poem above might seem 'wrong' to some people. Certainly, in current everyday speech it would sound flowery. Word order usually follows a conventional pattern. As children look at these sentences they may react differently to them. Some will be clear cut, others may need to be discussed further.

One way children could consider these sentences is to imagine they were teaching English. If they heard these constructions in a conversation in the classroom, which would they accept and which would they query?

Photocopiable: Word juggling
In this activity the children juggle with possible word orders. What is the maximum number of sentences that they can make with the set of words? Encourage them to see how particular words govern subsequent ones, taking care to ensure that the word order makes sense. (You may want to permit grammatical changes to words, for example allowing verb tenses to change or nouns to take '-s' endings.)

Photocopiable: Sentence changing
Invite the children to look at sentences they have used in their own writing in the past to see how the word order could be altered and improved.

Following up
Circling sentences: Ask the children to sit in a circle and tell a story, word by word. This will demonstrate the way in which particular words govern subsequent ones. The starter says the first word, the next child follows with the second word, and so on. For example, the starter may say 'A', which is then followed by 'short'… the next person then has to think carefully about which word to use – 'giant', for example, would not be appropriate.

Story sentences: The children can look at sentences in stories and see if they can devise alternative ways in which the same thing could have been said. They can look at places where the position of phrases containing adverbs and adjectives, for example, can be interchanged. This can work particularly well with the all-important, opening lines of stories (or is it 'With the all-important, opening lines of stories this can work particularly well?')

Parallel writing: Ask a child to perform a simple action, such as throwing a ball up into the air and catching it. Three children should watch the action, then each write three sentences about the action without showing one another what they have written. On completing these, they should share their sentences and see if they have written the same thing. If not, how did they differ? What words did they use differently? What word order variations in their sentences did they have?

Sounds right?

❏ Cut out these sentences. Say them aloud and listen to how they sound. Group together:

the sentences that sound like words in order

Made complete sense to me

the sentences that sound like words out of order

Made no sense to me

the sentences that make an odd sort of sense

Made an odd sort of sense to me

I am ill.	Played on I the swing.
Ill I am.	Ate I my toast.
I am ill.	The swing I played on.
I played on the swing.	My toast I ate.
I ate my toast.	I ill am.
Don't sit on the swing.	I the swing played on.
Ill am I.	I my toast ate.
The swing played on me.	On the swing don't sit.
My toast ate me.	Am I ill?
The swing don't sit on.	Ill, am I?
Am ill I.	Ate I my toast?

Word juggling

❑ On a sheet of paper write as many sentences as you can using the words in bin 1. (You don't need to use all the words in each sentence.)
❑ Do the same for bins 2, 3 and 4.
❑ Choose two favourite sentences to write under each bin.

1.
mat
scruffy
was
the
cat
on
my
red   sat
yesterday

2.
is   I   on
can   parrot
just
roof   see
our   the
sitting
my

3.
at   the   my
a   brilliant
baseball
friend
practising   is
throwing
piano   playing

4.
breath   a
bad   green
fiery   monster
I
dragon   helped
had   the
tempered   with

Sentence changing

❑ Look at some sentences you have used in your own story writing. Select **eight** sentences and write them in the boxes.

1	5
2	6
3	7
4	8

❑ Look at the 'Word tips' box. What changes could you make to your sentences to improve them? Write a different version of each sentence on a separate sheet of paper.

Word tips

1. Is the sentence clear?
2. Does it use the right verb?
3. Could I have used an adjective or an adverb?

Connectives

Objective
Understand the way in which clauses are connected

Language issues
Clauses are units of language including at least a subject and (usually) a verb. They can be parts of sentences or whole sentences. The space between clauses can be marked by connecting words or punctuation. For example, two clauses can be separated by a comma:
I went to school, I think.
Or a semicolon:
I went to school; that was my first mistake.

There are also connective words that can link clauses. Words like 'and', 'but' and 'because' link clauses together. For example:
I went to school and I regretted it.
or
I went to school, but I got out at home time.

There are four ways in which clauses can be connected. These are shown in the table below.

Ways of teaching
Variety is the spice of connection in language. An important aim is to develop children's awareness of a range of ways of connecting clauses and escape the endless uses of the word 'and' encountered in so many stories. With this in mind, the activities should be accompanied by children reviewing their own uses of connecting devices in their writing.

About the activities
Photocopiable: Connect
The sentences can be completed using the connectives given on the sheet. Some connectives will need to be used more than once, but encourage the children to choose as wide a variety as possible.

Photocopiable: Connective jobs
This activity, in which the children identify different types of connective and explain their usage, can be supplemented by the use of real leaflets from shops, libraries and so on.

Photocopiable: Clause shading
In this activity children look at the clause style of a classic author. As a class, compare E Nesbitt's writing with the style of some modern day writers.

Following up
Counting types: Provide the children with different types of texts and ask them to look through them carefully to see if certain connectives feature more in some texts than in others, for example they may find explanatory texts have more causal connections and narratives more temporal ones.

And: Focus on the use of the word 'and' – ask the children to look through their own uses of 'and' in their story writing. Could they have used a better alternative?

Type of connection	Addition	Opposition	Cause	Time
Function	words to add things	words to oppose things	things causing other things	the times when things happened
Examples	*and* *also*	*but* *however*	*because* *so* *therefore*	*then* *and then* *after*

Connect

Words can be used to connect two bits of a sentence together. Bits of a sentence that say something are called clauses.

❑ Look at these broken sentences and find a connecting word you think fits between the two clauses.
You could use the same word twice, if you need to.

Connecting words

also but however therefore
and so and then
after because then

We can't go out _____ it is raining.

Playtime was starting _____ we lined up.

We were all ready to go _____ a message came saying it was raining.

Our teacher said, "It is raining outside _____ it's indoor play."

I really wanted to go out _____ we had to stay in.

Playtime is fun, _____ playtime is healthy.

Staying in is miserable _____ we are allowed to read comics.

I read a funny comic _____ I read a football comic.

We played one game _____ playtime ended.

Our teacher came back _____ lessons started.

The rain has stopped _____ we can't go out.

We will go out _____ we have had our dinners.

Connective jobs

Clauses can be connected in different ways.

Some connecting words add clauses together.	Some connecting words oppose one clause against another.	Some connecting words show how one thing caused another
I like chips **and** I like them from the chip shop.	I like chips **but** I can't afford them.	I ate some chips **because** I was hungry.

or was caused by another.	Some connecting words show the times when things happened.
I was hungry **so** I bought some chips.	I had some chips, **then** I went and had some more.

❑ Look at the connecting words in this leaflet. Highlight them and point out the job they are doing.

The Space
Broom Street, Sheffield
the heart of the city

Outside, city life bustles on but inside the Space you can take a break. Attractions include:

Gallery: The central exhibition area currently houses touring art exhibitions and work by local artists. Works by Space artists are displayed then sold at our monthly art sale.

Artspace: A space where artists hold workshops. Children's art classes are run on Saturday morning, also during half-term holidays.

Café: After touring the exhibitions you can relax on the terrace café. Enjoy one of our range of cakes and drinks and then have another trip round the exhibition!

Drama classes: These will start next spring but are not running at present because of a lack of funding.

After school classes: In the coming term we will be starting after school art classes so we are currently offering places. Please ask at the front desk.

There is no charge for admission but we do encourage visitors to make a voluntary contribution of £1 so we can meet our running costs.

Clause shading

Clauses can be connected or separated by
- connecting words
- commas
- full stops.

❑ Look at this extract from a story over a hundred years old. Read the sentences and find the separate clauses and the way they are connected or separated.

> Remember, a clause is like a mini-sentence with its own verb.

Chapter 2

I am afraid the last chapter was rather dull. It is always dull in books when people talk and talk and don't do anything, but I was obliged to put it in, or else you wouldn't have understood all the rest. The best part of books is when things are happening. That is the best part of real things too. That is why I shall not tell you in this story about the days when nothing happened. You will not catch me saying, 'thus the sad days passed slowly by' – or 'the years rolled on their weary course' – or 'time went on' – because it is silly; of course time goes on – whether you say so or not. So I shall just tell you the nice, interesting parts – and in between you will understand that we had our meals and got up and went to bed, and dull things like that.

from The Treasure Seekers *by E Nesbitt*

Changing words

Contents of Term 3a

Unit 1: **Verb endings**	Learn the ways in which verbs and verb endings can change
Unit 2: **Comparitive endings**	Understanding the ways in which comparative endings change
Unit 3: **Pluralization**	Understand the ways in which noun endings change for plurals
Unit 4: **Change and word class**	Use changes that can be made in words to identify word class
Unit 5: **Changes**	Investigate particular ways in which words can and can't change

This half-term

This half-term looks at various types of word ending, including comparative endings and pluralization. Once again we are encountering features of grammar that are more than just spelling rules. They provide ways of looking at how certain word types, such as nouns and verbs, operate. Much of this unit involves changing one type of word to another and looking at how this affects the form of the word.

Poster notes

Verb masher
This is a large version of the chart used in Unit 1. It provides an opportunity for the class to suggest and use their own examples in the chart.

Plurals
The 'Plurals' poster shows the various ways words are altered to change a singular noun into a plural.

Verb masher

Base form	-s form	-ing participle	-ed past form

Plurals

Usual rule
The usual way of turning a singular noun to a plural is to add an **s**.
For example:

cat   →   *cats*
spoon   →   *spoons*

But if the singular ends in any of the following ways, then the plural is sometimes made in a different way.

Singular endings	Usual rule	Example
y after a consonant	Remove **y**, add **ies**	*fairy* → *fairies*
y after a vowel	add **s**	*day* → *days*
o after a consonant	add **es**	*potato* → *potatoes*
o after a vowel	add **s**	*video* → *videos*
with a sound like **s**, such as **ss**, **sh**, **tch**, **x**, **z**	add **es**	*kiss* → *kisses* *wish* → *wishes* *watch* → *watches*
ch sounding like it does at the end of 'perch'	add **es**	*perch* → *perches*
f	Remove **f**, add **ves***	*thief* → *thieves*

*(For some words nowadays, it is acceptable to retain the **f** and just add **s**, for example **roofs**.)

Verb endings

Objective
Learn the ways in which verbs and verb endings can change

Language issues
There are four common forms of verbs.
The plain form: *cook*.
The '-s' form used, at times, for the third-person singular: *he cooks, she cooks*.
The '-ing' participle indicating that the action is ongoing: *I was cooking, I am cooking, I will be cooking*.
The past tense '-ed' form: *I cooked*.

A number of verbs take these regular endings. However, there are some that don't. Interestingly enough they tend to be very important ones such as 'I am', 'I can', 'I do'.

Ways of teaching
Children need an understanding of the common forms verbs can take, coupled with an awareness that exceptions are rife. The activities in this unit present the exceptions as well as the rules.

About the activities
Photocopiable: Verb masher
This activity takes the children through the various endings that regular verbs can take. Remind them that if they find it difficult to work out what ending a verb should have, it is helpful to think of an example of its use. It is easier to think of the third-person use of the

word 'cook', for example, if you think of a context in which you would say the word, such as in the sentence 'He cooks in the kitchen'.

Photocopiable: Shaun's story
Various forms of verbs used in this story have been removed, leaving only the base form. The children have to write in the correct forms. Remind them to use the context to figure out how the base form should be altered. There are a number of irregular verbs in the story, so they will need to rely less on the rules, saying the sentences aloud to hear if they make sense.

Photocopiable: Make the change
The children are asked to fill in the tables in this activity to change the base form of the verb to the third person and to the past tense. Looking at the context of each sentence will help the children to provide the correct verb ending. This activity can be used as a starting point for looking at which verbs follow a rule and which do not.

Following up
Sorting verbs: Compile a large chart of verbs, asking the children to add more verbs as they encounter them. Divide the chart into two sections according to whether the verb takes on regular forms or irregular.

Dictionary forms: Ask the children to look through dictionaries to find verbs that follow a regular form. In many dictionaries the other forms of a verb are listed along with the base form.

Verb masher

One verb can appear in lots of different forms.

I kick

He kicks

I am kicking

I kicked

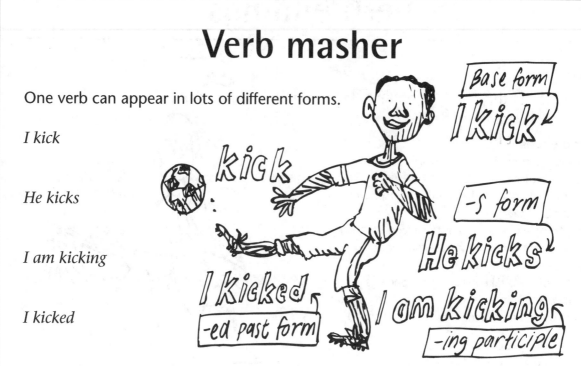

❑ Look at the verbs in the tray and write them out in the correct form in the verb masher. Look at some of the changes that happen. Are there times when changes you expect don't happen?

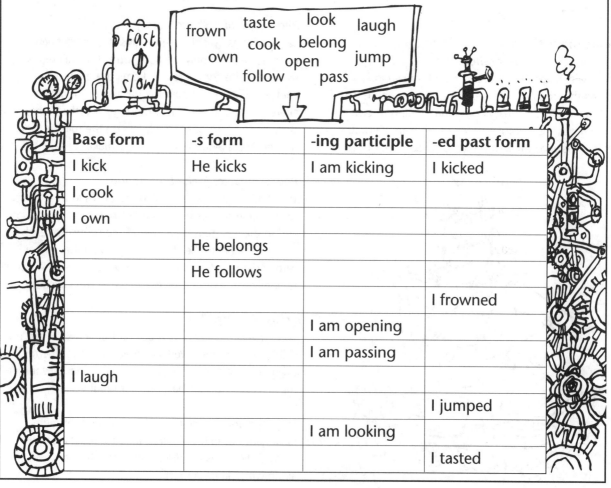

frown taste look laugh cook belong own open jump follow pass

Base form	-s form	-ing participle	-ed past form
I kick	He kicks	I am kicking	I kicked
I cook			
I own			
	He belongs		
	He follows		
			I frowned
		I am opening	
		I am passing	
I laugh			
			I jumped
		I am looking	
			I tasted

Shaun's story

❑ Look at this story. It contains verbs printed in the simple form. They need to be changed. Write the correct version over each verb (printed in italic), making sure that it fits in with the story.

Take care! Lots of these verbs change in different ways from the usual.

Yesterday I *go* to my grans. I go there every Wednesday after school. She *make* my tea and then we do the dishes. She *say* I do them much better than my grandad. We always make a cup of tea. I have orange juice and she *have* tea with one sugar. While we're *have* our drink she *tell* me a story.

Anyway, yesterday I *have* chips and we *do* the dishes. Then, after making the drinks, she *tell* me Grandad's secret.

"We *have* been married for thirty years," she said, "when one day we were *do* the dishes and I *see* him washing a plate. He *wash* it all, but left one bit. The washing brush *go* all round this one bit. I couldn't believe what I was *see* !"

"Suddenly, I *know* what he *have* been up to all these years." "He deliberately *leave* a bit! Whenever he *do* the washing up he left a bit. His idea was that if he *do* that, I wouldn't ask him to do it so often. So there I was, *stare* at him and he *look* at me. He *know* I *know* what he was up to. We didn't say a word. But I'm *tell* you... he never *do* it again!"

Make the change

❑ Fill in the spaces in each table.

❑ Change the verbs to the third person.

Every day I make my sandwiches.	Every day he _____ his sandwiches.
I only laugh at jokes if they are funny.	My brother only _____ at jokes if they are funny.
I have to do my homework now.	She _____ to do her homework now.
At the weekend I do some cleaning.	At the weekend he _____ some cleaning.
On Fridays I go to science club.	On Fridays she _____ to science club.
If I lose something I usually find it behind my bed.	If he loses something he usually _____ it behind his bed.
I like to read comics.	He _____ to read comics.
I am brilliant!	My mum _____ brilliant!

❑ Change the verbs to the past tense.

Every day I make my sandwiches.	Yesterday I _____ my sandwiches.
I only laugh at jokes if they are funny.	I _____ at the jokes because they were funny.
At the weekend I do some cleaning.	Last weekend I _____ some cleaning.
When I lose a sock I look for it.	When I _____ a sock I looked for it.
On Fridays I go to science club.	Last Friday I _____ to science club.
I like the clowns.	When we went to the circus I _____ the clowns.
I have to do my homework now.	Earlier on, I _____ to do my homework.
Today, school is brilliant!	Yesterday, school _____ brilliant!

❑ What do you notice about the changes to the verbs?

Comparative endings

Objective
Understand the ways in which comparative endings change

Language issues
Comparative and superlative forms of adjectives are usually made by adding 'er' and 'est' to the plain (or nominative) adjective, for example *sharp → sharper*. If the adjective ends in 'y' the 'y' is changed to 'i' before the addition is made, for example *happy → happier*.

   If the adjective consists of one syllable and there is only one vowel before the final consonant, then the final consonant is doubled before the ending is added, for example *sad → sadder*.

Ways of teaching
The initial activity looks at changes to adjective endings. These are then tried out within the contexts of reading and writing poetry and a critical reading of advertising.

About the activities
Photocopiable: Comparatives and superlatives
The notes about adjective endings in 'Language issues' (see above) are important here. The children can use this activity as a way of applying the rules as well as figuring out which words are exceptions. Conclude the activity by asking the children to check their answers with others in their group. Often other children will notice missed rules or odd results.

Photocopiable: Liars
Children can use shared reading to read the poem with their group, or the poem can be read in pairs. They could even act it out. Eventually the poem can be used as a model for writing their own 'liars' poem. They can use the same build-up of nominative, comparative and superlative but find their own adjectives. As with the original, they can take an idea and build around it using appropriate text.

Photocopiable: Advert words
Advert jingles such as 'Only the crumbliest, flakiest chocolate' make use of various forms of adjectives. Seek out examples of different adjectives used in adverts for the class to analyse, letting the children watch the adverts on television. Alternatively they can do the collecting task at home, finding examples in their evening viewing.

Following up
Adjective advertising: Ask the children to devise a slogan or jingle for a new product. They can draw upon their understanding of various adjective forms when they are producing their own example.

List the exceptions: The children can build up a list of adjectives to which the two rules apply – that is, those ending in 'y' and those where the final consonant needs to be doubled.

Comparatives and superlatives

Adjectives can take three forms. There is the plain adjective, sometimes called the **nominative**; the adjective that compares, the **comparative**; and the adjective that beats them all, the **superlative**.

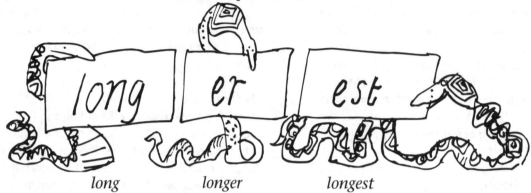

long   longer   longest

❏ Look at the adjectives in the table and fill in the missing spaces.

But remember – some could be irregular:

good   →   better   →   best

and some longer adjectives may take the other forms using **more** and **most**.

beautiful   →   more beautiful   →   most beautiful

Nominative	Comparative	Superlative
tall		
silly		
careful		
	shorter	
sad		
		happiest
		quietest
	more different	
cold		
	cooler	
	hotter	
		oldest
high		
	smaller	
		lowest

Liars

❏ Read the poem out loud in your group. You could each take one of the parts.
❏ Look for comparative and superlative adjectives. The poem contains some strange examples.

"I've got a tall cousin."
    "My cousin is taller."
"So! My other cousin is even taller."
    "Well, my second cousin is tallest!"

"My aunty is frightening."
    "My aunty is more frightening. She's so frightening
I don't even want to talk about it."
    "How frightening is that?"
    "Most frightening!"

"My bedroom is terrible."
    "My bedroom is terribler."
"My bedroom is terriblest."
    "Oh… right… Mine's just the most terrible."

"My gran is potty"
    "My gran is pottier."
"My gran is pottiest."
    "My gran potties the pottiest."

"My best friend is slimy."
    "My best friend is slimier."
"My friend's friend is the slimiest."
    "I know someone slimier than that."
"I'm not so sure. He is so slimy he can't walk without slipping!"
    "So! My second-best friend's so slimy he doesn't walk – he slithers!"
"I don't care – you're still my best friend."
    "How sweet."

"I'm a big liar."
    "I'm a bigger liar."
"I don't believe you."
    "Nor do I!"

❏ Now try to write your own poem using adjectives in the same way.

Advert words

❏ Find adverts in a newspaper or magazine.
Watch a few on the television.
Look for them on billboards.

❏ Look for nominative, comparative and superlative adjectives. Write some of the strings of words in this space.

Nominative	Comparative	Superlative

Pluralization

Objective
Understand the ways in which noun endings change for plurals

Language issues
The general idea of 'adding an "s" to make a plural' is subject to a number of exceptions. In many of the rules shown in the table below there are alterations that occur when the 's' is added. In addition to these, there are other pluralizations that are irregular, for example 'child' and 'children'. Other examples of exceptions include words such as 'sheep' and 'trousers', which do not change at all in the plural form.

Ways of teaching
The regularity of these rules is on the teacher's side when it comes to teaching pluralization. They provide clear help to children in forming plurals. The list in the table (see below) is also provided as a poster on photocopiable page 104 and is an invaluable guide to the pluralization of nouns.

About the activities
Photocopiable: Add an 's'?
Part of the skill employed by language users is the instinctive feel for what is correct. We are so immersed in its use we instinctively react to spellings or word forms that just don't sound right. This is a skill children will use as they try pluralizing the words given on the photocopiable sheet.

One approach to the activity is to go through the input section of the machine on the sheet as a class, putting an 's' at the end of each of the words. This will probably elicit the immediate reaction from the children that 'It doesn't look right' or 'We don't say "childs"!'

Photocopiable: Make the plural
As for the previous photocopiable, the children need to rely on what they feel is correct in an instinctive way when they choose the plural form of each word. In this activity, by eliminating the words that they know are wrong, the children may find it easier to decide on which word is correct.

Photocopiable: Random nouns
In this activity the children are asked to find nouns – any texts can be used – and change them from singular to plural or vice versa. Remind them to refer to the rules for plural endings (on the poster on photocopiable page 104), and to be aware that they are likely to encounter the pluralization of words that are exceptions to the rules.

Following up
Explain the error: Children can take the rules chart on the 'Plurals' poster on photocopoiable page 104 and use it as a way of reviewing their own spelling. If they have some writing they did in a previous year stored in a record folder, ask them to read through their work carefully to see where they missed out on certain rules.

New plurals: Looking at contemporary comics or pop and computer magazines, children can find new nouns, such as terms in computer jargon (for example, 'byte') or words that are creeping into general speech (for example, 'geek'), and form their plurals.

Some established rules

Singular endings	Usual rule	Example	
'y' after a consonant	Remove 'y', add 'ies'	fairy	→ fairies
'y' after a vowel	add 's'	day	→ days
'o' after a consonant	add 'es'	potato	→ potatoes
'o' after a vowel	add 's'	video	→ videos
with a sound like 's', such as 'ss', 'sh', 'tch', 'x', 'z'	add 'es'	kiss	→ kisses
		wish	→ wishes
		watch	→ watches
'ch' sounding like it does at the end of 'perch'	add 'es'	perch	→ perches
'f'	Remove 'f', add 'ves'	thief	→ thieves

Add an 's'?

The rule we often use to make a plural is 'add an **s**'.

❑ Look at the nouns in the plural sorter. Sort the ones that follow the 'add **s**' rule from the ones that don't. Write down the plural words in the correct section of the machine.

van   man
path   bus   tooth   fish
trousers   child   woman
sheep   wish
tree   sister   box   knife
glass   foot   boot
leaf   fence   wolf
shop   plate

'add **s**'

'another rule'

Make the plural

❑ Read the poster for making plurals.

❑ Look at these singular nouns. Each is followed by three possible plurals. Circle the correct plural for each noun.

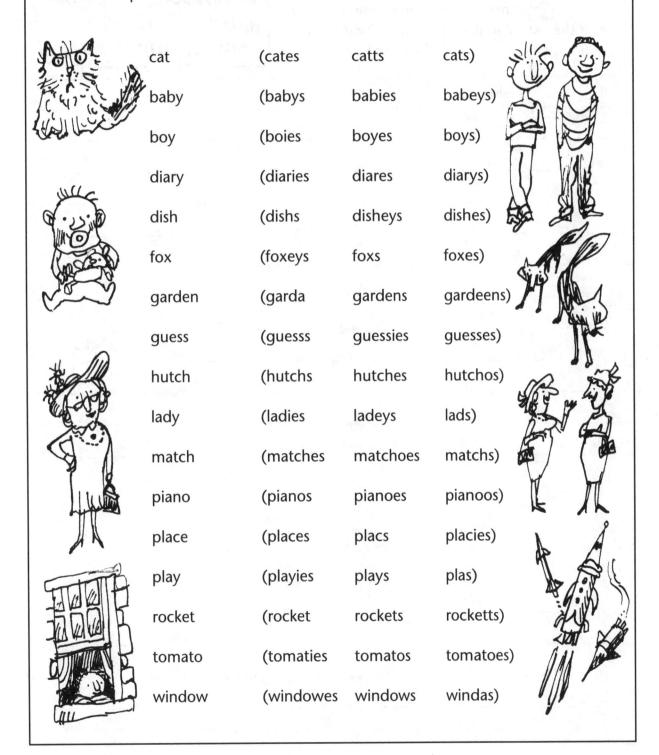

cat	(cates	catts	cats)
baby	(babys	babies	babeys)
boy	(boies	boyes	boys)
diary	(diaries	diares	diarys)
dish	(dishs	disheys	dishes)
fox	(foxeys	foxs	foxes)
garden	(garda	gardens	gardeens)
guess	(guesss	guessies	guesses)
hutch	(hutchs	hutches	hutchos)
lady	(ladies	ladeys	lads)
match	(matches	matchoes	matchs)
piano	(pianos	pianoes	pianoos)
place	(places	placs	placies)
play	(playies	plays	plas)
rocket	(rocket	rockets	rocketts)
tomato	(tomaties	tomatos	tomatoes)
window	(windowes	windows	windas)

Random nouns

❑ Take any text. It could be a story, a newspaper article, an advert or an information book.

Read a chunk from it, finding the first **twenty** nouns. Write them in the correct column, then:
- If they are singular write their plural form.
- If they are plural write their singular form.

Remember, nouns can usually be changed from singular to plural.

singular	plural

Change and word class

Objective
Use changes that can be made in words to identify word class

Language issues
The various changes words can undergo and the relationships they form within a sentence can provide us with ways of recognizing which words perform which function. To test for:

❑ a noun – can the word be pluralized? (Most nouns alter if they are changed from the singular to the plural.)
❑ a verb – can the word have its tense changed? (Most verbs alter as the tense of their phrase alters.)
❑ an adjective – does it modify the noun?
❑ an adverb – does it modify the verb?
❑ a pronoun – can the word be replaced by a noun?

Ways of teaching
These simple tests are bound to fail for certain words. For example, 'Paris' is a noun. Applying the plural test generates 'Parises'. The oddities remind us that the rules are only generalized ones, but they are ones that children can use, none the less.

About the activities
Photocopiable: Wordsorts
Ask the children to test the words (using the rules given on the sheet) to highlight the different types of words used in the passage.

Photocopiable: Top ten parts
In this activity the children find lyrics from chosen songs and look at the language used. Pop songs often take on distinctive uses of language. An example from the not too distant past includes Des'ree's use of adjectives in *You Gotta Be.*

• *You gotta be bad* • *You gotta be bold* • *You gotta be wiser* • *You gotta be hard* • *You gotta be tough* • *You gotta be stronger* • *You gotta be cool, you gotta be calm, you gotta stay together…*

Photocopiable: Your definitions
Children who have had experience of working with the various types of word – noun, verb, adjective and adverb – can, in this activity, set down their own definitions and examples. Their examples may include material from the previous activity or other current in-vogue material.

Following up
Parts in sentences: Ask the children to try writing sentences that contain a noun, verb, adjective, adverb and pronoun. They can write the different types of words in different colours for easy identification.

Talkers: Can the children think of anyone on television whose speech is particularly noticeable? It could be someone who whinges all the time or talks too quickly. They can listen to the speech of this person and see what types of word dominate their speech.

Adjective and adverb hunt: Children can aim to find 100 adjectives or adverbs in texts around them. These could be on posters or notices, in newspaper and magazine headlines or in leaflets.

Wordsorts

Here are some ways of detecting some of the different types of word in use.

If the word can change from a singular to a plural, it could be a **noun**.	If the word or phrase can be switched from one tense to another, it could be a **verb**.	If the word or phrase is adding to the meaning of the noun, it could be an **adjective**.	If the word or phrase is altering the meaning of the verb, it could be an **adverb**.	If a particular word can be replaced by a noun it could be a **pronoun**.

❏ Using these rules, try to find the different types of word in this story. Circle the different types of word in different colours.

I know someone who went on a fishing trip. He took his old grandad with him. The boat was a rickety little one. The trip was great, but the weather started to get windy. The boat started rocking violently. They wondered if they should quickly turn back but Grandad said they should definitely carry on. He desperately wanted to catch a fish. Just then he foolishly leaned over the side and his false teeth fell into the water. He was really annoyed and this made him utterly determined to go on until they caught a fish.

After an hour on this rough sea it looked as if Grandad had finally caught a really big fish. But the fish quickly bit the fishing line and got away. The fish slowly bobbed up to the side of the boat and lifted its eyes out of the murky water. There, in its little mouth, they could see Grandad's false teeth.

PHOTOCOPIABLE

Top ten parts

❏ Copy out the words to the chorus or the main lines from a current pop song.

❏ Look at the language used. Look at the number of different types of word.
Look at the way the words are arranged.
Write a few comments about the language of the pop song.

_____

_____

_____

_____

Your definitions

❑ Write your own brief definitions of the different types of word, and give some examples for each one. The first one has been started for you.

Remember to note anything significant about the words – such as odd endings and changes.

Remember to include any interesting points from current usage or other languages you speak or have encountered.

Noun	Verb	Adjective	Adverb
the name you would call a thing			
Examples	Examples	Examples	Examples
the sun			

Changes

Objective
Investigate particular ways in which words can and can't change

Language issues
There are four basic types of sentence. *Declarative* sentences make a statement, for example, 'The car is slow'. *Interrogative* sentences ask a question or are phrased in a questioning way, for example, 'Is the car slow?' or 'The car is slow?' *Imperative* sentences issue commands and orders, for example, 'Slow down!' *Exclamatory* sentences make an exclamation and express the emotion of the speaker in the form of an outburst, for example, 'Wow, that's slow!'

Ways of teaching
The four basic sentence types tend to have different numbers of words or different word orders. They can also be marked by different forms of punctuation. In some cases, saying the sentence aloud can give children an idea of the different forms.

About the activities
Photocopiable: Sentence types
Focusing on the definitions of sentence types, this activity presents sentences which all have similar vocabulary but perform different functions.

Photocopiable: Question shuffles
Through 'playing with' the words that they cut out, the children will be able to take the statements and turn them into questions. They could then try to make imperative or exclamatory sentences. Stress the

importance of looking at the word order when they are making the changes. Are there any common changes? They can also look at words that are left out when they form the other types of sentence.

Photocopiable: Looking at changes
This activity focuses on making changes to sentences – the changes required are relatively straightforward – and then moving on to mark the altered words, the changes to word order and the additional words.

Following up
Shuffling: The children can cut out words from newspaper headlines and try to make their own statements that can be shuffled into questions or imperatives. Remind them that they will need to change word endings, and provide them with extra lettering.

Top titles: Looking at lists of best-selling books, videos or popular songs (such as the top ten sales charts featured in some newspapers), children can analyse the titles to look for any that are declarative, interrogative, imperative or exclamatory.

Cartoon speech: In comic stories the speech is often short and snappy and it will often include a wide range of examples of imperative and exclamatory sentences. Ask the children to look through a comic-strip story, reading the speech bubbles to see which types of sentences they can find.

Sentence types

There are four basic types of sentence.

A declarative sentence: *The car is slow.*
Definition: A sentence that states something.

An interrogative sentence: *Is the car slow?*
Definition: A sentence that asks something.

An imperative sentence: *Slow down!*
Definition: A sentence that gives an order.

An exclamatory sentence: *Wow, that's slow!*
Definition: A sentence that exclaims. (For example, the person sounds surprised.)

❏ Cut out out these sentences and sort them into the four different types. Then paste them in their separate sets onto a large sheet of paper. Give each set a heading – declarative, interrogative, imperative and exclamatory.

❏ Add your own examples, too. Write them on separate strips of paper and place them in the correct sets.

Is this cat fierce?	Tea made yet?	We made a mess.
What a mess!	Who made this mess?	Make the tea.
This cat is fierce.	Tea's ready!	That's one fierce cat!
Clear up this mess.	Take care of the cat.	The tea is made.

Question shuffles

❑ These words have been placed into sentences. They are all statements.
Cut them out, then shuffle them around to make questions.

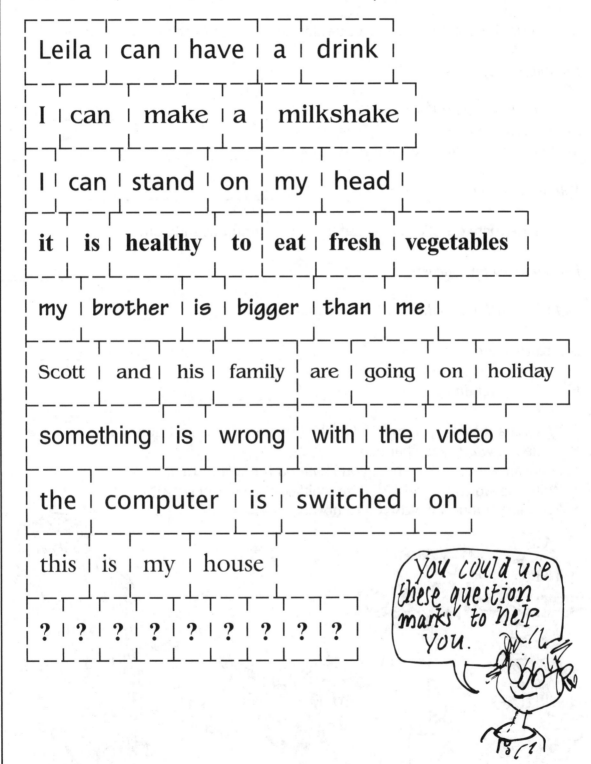

| Leila | can | have | a | drink |

| I | can | make | a | milkshake |

| I | can | stand | on | my | head |

| **it** | **is** | **healthy** | **to** | **eat** | **fresh** | **vegetables** |

| **my** | **brother** | **is** | **bigger** | **than** | **me** |

| Scott | and | his | family | are | going | on | holiday |

| something | is | wrong | with | the | video |

| the | computer | is | switched | on |

| this | is | my | house |

| ? | ? | ? | ? | ? | ? | ? | ? | ? |

You could use these question marks to help you.

Looking at changes

❏ Look at the sentences below. Can you change the statements into questions and the questions into statements?

❏ Change these statements into questions, writing out each one.

I found my keys. _____

We don't have PE on Friday. _____

My mum went to stay with my gran. _____

You like bananas. _____

❏ Change these questions into statements, writing out each one.

Do you know my teacher? _____

Did you play basketball? _____

Is it teatime yet? _____

Has it stopped raining? _____

❏ What changes did you make? On the first statements and questions:
• Circle the words you changed.
• Draw arrows to show where you changed the word order.
• Write the words you added. (Use a different coloured pencil.)
• Put a line through words you removed.

Organizing sentences

Contents of Term 3b

This half-term

In this half-term, various features of sentences are revisited or looked at for the first time. Much of the focus is on the organizing of sentences, whether through the use of appropriate punctuation or the use of particular connectives.

Poster notes

Colon and *Semicolon*
These two posters explain how colons and semicolons are used, and can be referred to throughout Units 2 and 3.

One of the most effective ways of developing children's understanding of these punctuation marks is to ask them to devise their own examples of sentences in which they are used.

Colon

Colons are used to introduce lists:

For this experiment you will need: a glass of water, a teaspoon of salt.

or summaries:

We have learned the following: salt dissolves in water...

or examples:

Some materials dissolve, for example: salt in water, sugar in coffee.

or quotations:

My teacher always says: "The colon is a funny little mark."

Colons introduce second clauses that expand or illustrate the first:

The water evaporated: it turned into water vapour.

It separates one clause from another, without cutting the two off like a full stop.

The colon is a funny little mark.

Semicolon

Semicolons can separate two closely linked clauses:

The water evaporated; I said it would.

They show there is some link between the two things separated:

Salt dissolves in water; sugar does too.

They can be used to separate complicated items in a list (where a comma won't do the job so well):

Our saucers contained salt, water and sugar; salt and water; sugar and water; water on its own.

Semicolons are stronger than commas, but weaker than full stops.

Revisiting punctuation

Objective
Identify common punctuation marks

Language issues
One of the chief reasons punctuation is used is because it clarifies reading. The words in the following sentence show this at work:

Laura was sound asleep an hour after she walked into school.
When punctuated, this sentence reads:
Laura was sound asleep. An hour after, she walked into school.

Ways of teaching
The focus of the activities in this unit is on finding the places in a text where punctuation marks should be inserted. Experiencing the difficulty of reading without punctuation is followed by the children looking at different ways in which it can be used.

About the activities
Photocopiable: Finding punctuation
The children can try reading the unpunctuated version of this passage before reading the punctuated one. Looking at the confusions that arise and trying to make sense of the text will help the children to realize that without punctuation certain sections of the passage may be misread.

Photocopiable: Find and explain
Following on from the reading of 'David's omelettes', children can look for various punctuation marks in the first, punctuated version of the text. In some cases they will have looked at the rules for using a particular punctuation mark, for instance the apostrophe. In others they will need to look closely at particular sentences in the passage to try to gauge the purpose of individual punctuation marks.

Photocopiable: Punctuation hunt
This activity encourages the children to familiarize themselves with various forms of punctuation by reading text in newspapers and magazines. Some children may need help in clarifying the task that a particular punctuation mark is performing once they have identified it in the text.

Following up
Popular punctuation marks: Children can look at different texts to see if there are any punctuation marks that appear more in some than in others. Comic stories can contain a fair quota of exclamation marks; application forms usually have many question marks.

Race to find: Give the children a three-minute challenge. Explain that, working in groups of three with newspaper cuttings, they have to try to find as many punctuation marks as they can within the time-limit.

Estimate: Show a block of text to the children from a distance or projected out of focus on an OHP. Ask them to estimate how many full stops or speech marks they think it may contain. Having made their estimates they can then see the text close-up or in focus to check how accurate they were.

Finding punctuation

David's omelettes

David makes brilliant omelettes. David's recipe uses the following: two eggs, a little bit of butter, grated cheese and one finely chopped mushroom (it has to be chopped into really little bits and fried beforehand).

First take an egg-beater and beat the eggs; they don't need to be very well beaten. Then melt the butter in a small frying pan (don't let the butter get too hot!). Pour the beaten egg mixture into the pan. When it is nearly solid, turn it over and sprinkle the mushrooms over it. Then quickly add the grated cheese and fold the omelette into the shape of a semicircle. Let the cheese melt for a few moments; take care the omelette doesn't overcook.

David says, "A good omelette is not a snack. My recipe – it's a meal in itself." What do you think?

davids omelettes

david makes brilliant omelettes davids recipe uses the following two eggs a little bit of butter grated cheese and one finely chopped mushroom it has to be chopped into really little bits and fried beforehand

first take an egg beater and beat the eggs they dont need to be very well beaten then melt the butter in a small frying pan dont let the butter get too hot pour the beaten egg mixture into the pan when it is nearly solid turn it over and sprinkle the mushrooms over it then quickly add the grated cheese and fold the omelette into a the shape of a semicircle let the cheese melt for a few moments take care the omelette doesnt overcook

david says a good omelette is not a snack my recipe its a meal in itself what do you think

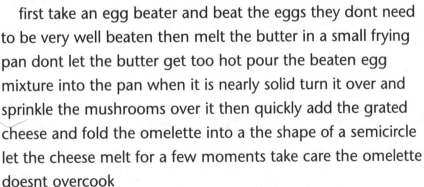

Find and explain

❏ Read 'David's omelettes'. Look for these punctuation marks. Circle them in the passage.

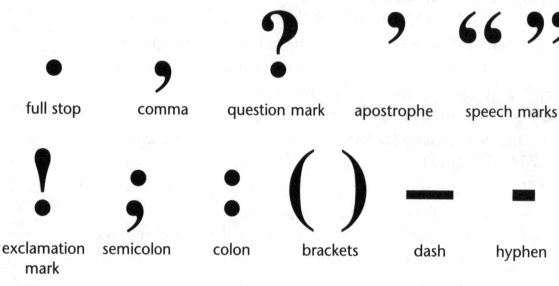

full stop   comma   question mark   apostrophe   speech marks

exclamation mark   semicolon   colon   brackets   dash   hyphen

❏ In the boxes put a tick each time you find one of them.

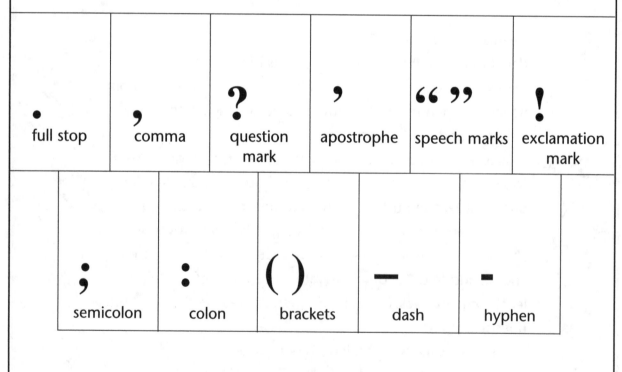

• full stop	' comma	? question mark	' apostrophe	" " speech marks	! exclamation mark

; semicolon	: colon	( ) brackets	— dash	- hyphen

❏ Explain what job they are doing on a separate piece of paper.

Punctuation hunt

❑ Look through a magazine and collect examples of **five** different types of punctuation. Cut out the pieces of text and paste them into the boxes. Write an explanation of what the punctuation marks are doing underneath the cuttings.

THE PRIME MINISTER SAID: "WE PLAN TO BUILD A CLEAR, BRIGHT, POSITIVE FUTURE."

comma – separating items in a list

Colon and semicolon

Objective

Recognize colons and semicolons and respond to them when reading

Language issues

Colons are used to introduce lists:
For this experiment you will need: a glass of water, a teaspoon of salt.

or summaries:
We have learned the following: salt dissolves in water...

or examples:
Some materials dissolve, for example: salt in water, sugar in coffee.

or quotations:
My teacher always says: 'The colon is a funny little mark.'

Colon's introduce second clauses that expand or illustrate the first:
The water evaporated: it turned into water vapour.
It separates one clause from another, without cutting the two off like a full stop.

Semicolons can separate two closely linked clauses:
The water evaporated; I said it would.

They show there is some link between the two things separated:
Salt dissolves in water; sugar does too.

and can be used to separate complicated items in a list (where a comma won't do the job so well):
Our saucers contained salt, water and sugar; salt and water; sugar and water; water on its own.
Semicolons are stronger than commas, but weaker than full stops.

Ways of teaching

Both these punctuation marks are classic examples of that great rule of punctuation: if in doubt, leave it out. However, when looking at some of the examples above, it is clear they serve a useful purpose. Without the semicolon in the last example, the text would read:
Our saucers contained salt, water and sugar, salt and water, sugar and water, water on its own.
The semicolon acts as a step above the comma.

This unit can be used as a springboard for children recognizing the two punctuation marks in their reading.

About the activities

Photocopiable: Colon and semicolon

The text on this sheet, explaining the ways that colons and semicolons can be used, links to the examples on the following photocopiable.

This photocopiable can also be used as a frame for children to devise their own examples for the various uses of the two punctuation marks.

Photocopiable: Examples – colons and semicolons

Having read the colon and semicolon sheet (photocopiable page 133), children can try to find one example of each type of their use. Give them plenty of time to read the examples given on photocopiable page 134, looking at the functions the colons and semicolons are performing, before trying to match them to the text given on page 133. Encourage them to use all the examples on the sheet as a model for trying to produce their own sample sentences containing colons and semicolons. Ask them to choose three of their own sentences and explain why they used colons or semicolons.

Photocopiable: Colon or semicolon?

Children insert the punctuation mark they believe to be appropriate using the examples in the previous activity as a guide. The examples are closely modelled on each other so, having completed this activity, it would be a good idea to ask them to look through some of the books in the classroom to find other, more varied uses of the colon and semicolon.

Following up

Writing type: Both these punctuation marks perform a particular role in certain types of writing, for example they can clarify the explanation of a science task or the listing of items used in a technology project. As these punctuation marks are introduced to the children, look at texts across the curriculum, focusing on writing in which their use could be reinforced.

Quotes book: Ask the children to include colons when recording quotations in a 'quotes book'. They can staple some pages of A5 paper together and, over a period of time, record the words members of their family and people in their neighbourhood are renowned for saying.

Colon and semicolon

Meet two new types of punctuation…

Colon :

Used to introduce a list

or a summary

or an example

or a quotation.

Introduces a second clause that explains the first.

Semicolon ;

Used to separate two closely linked clauses.

Shows there is some link between the two things it separates.

Can be used to separate complicated items in a list (where a comma won't do the job so well).

Examples – colons and semicolons

❑ Cut out the examples and match them to the explanations.

My teacher always says: "The colon is a funny little mark."

We have learned the following: salt dissolves in water…

The water evaporated; I said it would.

Salt dissolves in water; sugar does too.

Our saucers contained salt, water and sugar; salt and water; sugar and water; water on its own.

The water evaporated: it turned into water vapour.

For this experiment you will need: a glass of water, a teaspoon of salt.

Some materials dissolve, for example: salt in water, sugar in coffee

For this experiment you will need: a glass of water, a teaspoon of salt, three tadpoles and a small child.

Colon or semicolon?

❑ Look at these twelve sentences. In each there is a space. Should it have a colon or a semicolon?

1 There are some things that annoy me ☐ my little brother, my teacher, nasty dogs.

2 I like playtime ☐ Josh does too.

3 My grandad always says ☐ "Mind your manners, young lad."

4 This story teaches us the lesson ☐ don't count your chickens before they're hatched.

5 My pet snail packed his shell, said goodbye and slithered away ☐ he left!

6 Playtime was cancelled ☐ we were not pleased!

7 It was raining at playtime ☐ yesterday was the same.

8 Here is what you need ☐ an egg, a candle, a piece of string.

❑ Pick two of your sentences and explain why you chose the mark you used.

Sentence number _____ I used a _____ because _____ _____ _____ _____ _____	Sentence number _____ I used a _____ because _____ _____ _____ _____

Further use of colons and semicolons

Objective
Identify the function of colons and semicolons

Language issues
It is essential that language users understand *why* certain punctuation marks are used. Children can be guided by a set of rules when using colons and semicolons, but they will find them easier to understand and to incorporate in their own writing if the rules are supported by clear examples of the punctuation marks in use.

Ways of teaching
This unit looks at some of the uses of colons and semicolons and asks the children to decide which mark is most appropriate in particular sentences.

About the activities

Photocopiable: The Elves and the Shoemaker
This text contains a number of colons and semicolons – more than writers would use today. Ask the children to read the story in groups, looking closely at how the colons and semicolons are being used. Where would they *not* have used them if the text had been written by themselves today? Help them understand the functions that the punctuation marks (colons and semicolons) are performing in each context. They should consider the way these marks prompt them to pause – how different are they from full stops?

It is interesting to see how colons and semicolons have 'separated out' from each other in their usage in modern writing, having much more clearly defined functions. In 'The Elves and the Shoemaker' many of the colons would be substituted for a dash today (for example, 'At last he had nothing left in the world but a small piece of leather – just enough to make one final pair of shoes' or 'As for the shoemaker – he lived well the rest of his life'). Other colons would be replaced by full stops, especially in writing for young children ('We must do something for them. We shall make them some clothes and boots to keep them warm'), or semicolons ('Each night the shoemaker cut out his shoes; each morning he returned to find them expertly finished').

Photocopiable: Find and explain
Children can root through classroom texts and record the uses of colons and semicolons, noting the function they are performing in the context of the sentences. Explain the example given on the sheet before the children start their 'research'.

Photocopiable: Placing and choosing
This activity involves identifying where an appropriate punctuation mark could be placed in a sentence. One variation is to allow children two placings if they are not absolutely sure where the colon or semicolon should be inserted – they can place the punctuation mark once where they think it is most likely to go and then take a second guess, written above the line. It is important to point out to the children that a sentence may contain more than one colon or semicolon.

Following up
Usage survey: Is the semicolon dead? Ask the children to gather together texts from the present day and older texts, such as E Nesbit stories and poems by classic writers. They can survey these texts to see if semicolons are more in evidence or less in evidence than in modern texts. Children could conduct a survey of the use of semicolons by adults – do they ever use the semicolon, or indeed, are there some people who do not know when to use it?

Science: With its use in specific terms and at the start of a list, the colon is a punctuation mark that can be used in any writing that requires clear explanation, as in scientific writing (see the 'Writing type' following-up activity on page 132). Children could look through pieces of science work they have completed to see where they could have used this mark. They could also set themselves a target of trying to use it in future.

The Elves and the Shoemaker

❏ Use of punctuation changes over time. Sometimes older texts, like this one by the Brothers Grimm, contain more punctuation marks than modern texts. Read the story, find the colons and semicolons and look at how they are being used.

There was once an honest shoemaker who worked very hard; but no matter how much he worked, he never earned enough to live. At last he had nothing left in the world but a small piece of leather: just enough to make one final pair of shoes. The shoemaker cut the shoes out carefully and laid them out on his bench; they would be ready for when he returned in the morning. That night he said his prayers as usual and slept peacefully.

What a surprise greeted him next day: there on the workbench, was the most beautiful pair of shoes the shoemaker had ever seen! Every stitch was perfect; the craftsmanship was faultless. Later that day a gentleman came into the shop and asked to try the shoes. Imagine: they fitted him perfectly and he was so pleased that he payed handsomely for them. Now the shoemaker could buy more leather.

And so the days continued. Each night the shoemaker cut out his shoes: each morning he returned to find them expertly finished. He began to grow prosperous again.

One evening around Christmas time, the shoemaker made a decision: 'I want to stay up tonight,' he said to his wife, 'to see just who is making my shoes for me.' So they hid themselves in the workroom and waited.

At the stroke of midnight they heard the sound of tiny feet scuttling across the floor: two, tiny, naked men scrambled up to the shoemaker's bench, where they sat and began to sew and stitch the pieces of leather; working so swiftly that in no time at all they had finished the shoes. Then the two little men disappeared as quickly as they had come.

The shoemaker and his wife were astonished: they had never imagined that elves had been helping them. 'Those two little men have made us wealthy, husband,' said the wife. 'We must do something for them: we shall make them some clothes and boots to keep them warm.'

When the little men came that night, they fell on the clothing with delight; they quickly dressed themselves and danced and capered about the workroom – and right out of the door, never to be seen again.

As for the shoemaker: he lived well the rest of his life.

retold by Jackie Andrews

Find and explain

❑ Look in some texts for examples of colons and semicolons. Copy out sentences that contain the marks, and explain how they are being used.

Example	Explanation
The choir sang: "Sail forth! Steer for the deep waters only."	Colon used to introduce a quotation.
Example	Explanation
Example	Explanation
Example	Explanation
Example	Explanation

Placing and choosing

❑ Read the sentences below. Decide where you could place a punctuation mark. Choose the correct one – either a colon or a semicolon – and add it to the text.

When we go on the trip you will need the following a coat, a rucksack, packed lunch, sturdy shoes.

You can use capital letters to show names, for example Denmark, Dionne.

Ms Cooper always says this "The quicker you tidy the quicker you go."

The school day ended the bell rang and we were sent home.

Having considered all the arguments we have reached the following conclusion smoking is bad for your health.

Here are some things teachers say "Line up," "Sit down," "Be quiet."

Humpty sat on a wall he was taking a risk.

We walked home through the park it was our short cut.

Try making three new colours using red and yellow red, yellow and a bit of white red, yellow and a bit of blue.

Assembly was too long otherwise the morning was brilliant.

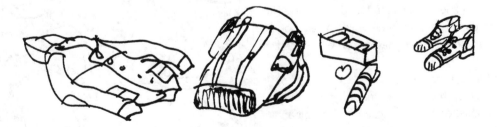

Hyphens and dashes

Objective
Identify and begin to understand the use of hyphens and dashes

Language issues
Hyphens and dashes can be used in various ways and historically there are some obscure rules, particularly those governing the use of the hyphen. The simplest guidance is that hyphens are used to join together two parts of a word into one. So, 'short' and 'sighted' become the single word 'short-sighted'.

The dash is an informal and increasingly common punctuation mark that can be used to insert words that clarify or interject into a sentence, for example:

My gran – who is eighty – plays football.
I looked around and – thankfully – there were my keys.

The dash can also tag bits onto a sentence:

Meet me at four – don't be late.

Dashes are often used instead of other marks such as commas, which could have been used in the first two examples above.

Ways of teaching
The distinction between the dash and hyphen is an important one. They perform different functions. Children will be able to find examples of hyphenated words in any texts and will also encounter the dash used in many types of writing.

About the activities
Photocopiable: Link words
This activity plays upon children's familiarity with various words they may not even have realized were hyphenated. In this way it introduces the types of word in which hyphens are used.

Photocopiable: Letter lines
The informality of a letter between friends lends itself to the use of the dash. In this example children can look at the text carefully to see where dashes can be inserted.

Photocopiable: Sports day
This activity plays with the idea of mock hyphenated words, asking children to construct a list of imaginary activities for a sports day using hyphenated words.

Following up
Create words: Children can use the hyphen as a way of creating new words to add to the language. They can start with a simple noun, verb or adjective and see if they can make new words that could make sense.

Finding hyphens: Ask the children to use a dictionary to find various words with hyphens. They can also compare different dictionaries – words will be hyphenated in some but not in others. Explain that over time, hyphenated words can lose their hyphen (for example, 'haystack').

Shop words: Looking through the local yellow pages, the children can find some examples of hyphenated business names. These could include some interesting features of language play (for example 'Toy-u-like' or 'CD-4-U').

Link words

Hyphens can connect compound words together.

❑ Look at the two sets of words below. Cut out the different halves of the words and join them up to create hyphenated words.

Sixty- could go with *four*, for example.

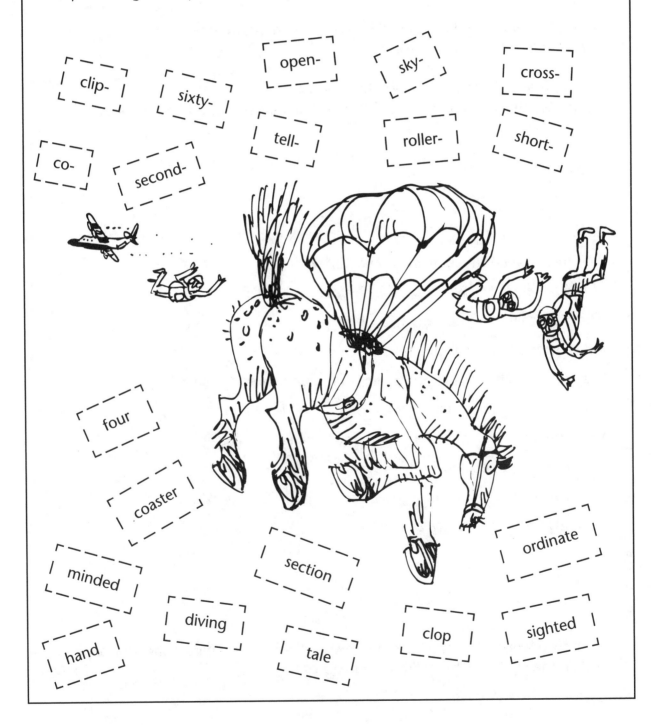

clip-   sixty-   open-   sky-   cross-

co-   second-   tell-   roller-   short-

four

coaster

minded   section   ordinate

diving   clop   sighted

hand   tale

Letter lines

Dashes can be used to slot things into sentences. (Commas can be used in a similar way.)

Annie – my sister – starts Nursery today.

Dashes tag things onto sentences:

Don't forget to bring a packed lunch for the trip – no glass bottles!

Dashes are often used to punctuate sentences in informal notes and letters.

I've got to go now – see ya' soon!

❑ Here is a letter from one friend to another.
Put the dashes where they should go. Each sentence could have one or two.

Dear Jack,

Just a few bits of news not in any order.

We miss you at school come back.

Ms Cooper who is sixty this year is retiring.

She is going to arrange a big party so she says.

Mr Harper our school nurse told me to say 'Hello' to you.

I am now the best footballer in our class I think.

Our garden swing the old rusty one is falling down.

My mum is coming home from my gran's can't wait to see her.

Tomorrow it's science my favourite lesson.

On Saturday I'm going to London just for a day.

Got to go now write soon.

Sam

❑ Choose four of the sentences and rewrite them on a separate sheet of paper.
Explain the jobs that the dashes are doing.

Sports day

❑ Copy the words from the box, arranging them in different orders and putting in hyphens to create some new games for a sports day.
For example: *balance-the-shark*

eat	the	shark
throw	a	teacher
balance	my	elephant
hunt	your	bus
chase	an	egg

The games

❑ What would the games involve?
❑ Could you invent some rules?
Write some notes on the back of this sheet.

Connectives to structure an argument

Objective
Investigate the use of connectives to structure an argument

Language issues
Arguments can be structured in particular ways. There are some connectives that develop arguments and reason how one thing leads to another, for example: 'We need more taxes *so that* we can pay for hospitals.' (See Unit 5 in Term 1b.) Particular connectives, such as 'finally' and 'clearly', can be used to sum up an argument, for example: 'Finally it is clear…'

Ways of teaching
This unit looks at some of the language uses associated with developing an argument. It can lead to children developing a frame or outline of how an argument can be structured; the critical aspect of these activities is that they focus on the sentence structures and words that could facilitate this.

About the activities
Photocopiable: Reasoning with connectives
This activity gives the children an opportunity to develop mini arguments. The frame that is given for the structuring of the arguments will reinforce their understanding of how connectives link phrases or sentences together. In their presentation of a case, children can be as wild and weird with their ideas as they wish, provided they can reason them through!

Photocopiable: Links
The protest leaflet develops clear links between one thing and another. The children can look through the language of the leaflet to find the way in which the argument is structured.

Photocopiable: Design and protest
Using the type of argument they have examined in the previous activity, children can devise their own leaflets.

Following up
Leaflets: Ask the children to collect various leaflets presenting arguments and to look for the way in which they are structured. Are there any differences?

Speeches: Video-record some speeches or interviews on the news for the children to watch. How do the participants of the debate use connectives to try to reason and 'connect' their arguments?

Debate: Encourage the children to structure an argument for or against a particular idea, such as 'the need for later bedtimes', 'all schools should have the same uniform' or 'playtimes should be abolished and the school day shortened'.

Reasoning with connectives

❑ Think of things you would argue for (**I think…**)
and give a reason for them (**because…**)
then sum up your argument (**Therefore…**).

Like this…

> **I think** playtime should be longer
> **because** if we play a lot we are ready to concentrate in class.
> **Therefore** we should play more so we will work more.

❑ Try your own.

Mini argument about

I think _____

because _____

Therefore _____

Mini argument about

I think _____

because _____

Therefore _____

Mini argument about

I think _____

because _____

Therefore _____

Mini argument about

I think _____

because _____

Therefore _____

Mini argument about

I think _____

because _____

Therefore _____

Links

In a lot of arguments things are connected together, showing that one thing causes another, or one thing will lead to another.

❑ Look at this protest leaflet and find some connections.

SAY NO TO THE NEW HOUSES!

Developers have been surveying Colley Woods because they are planning to build new houses there!

This will increase traffic through our village, but also it will destroy the wood. The initial plan is to build 30 houses, then 50 bungalows.
Say "No" to the developers and save our countryside.
If they build on Colley Woods then we will lose a beautiful, old woodland.

They say they want to provide new homes, but we say you should care for the countryside.

They say "develop", but we say "care".

Come to a meeting so that we can organize our protest.
Village Hall, Wed 30 Feb, 7.00pm.

We need to speak up now because tomorrow could be too late!

Design and protest

❑ Think of a cause you could champion:

less cars on the roads?
better parks and playgrounds?

❑ Devise a leaflet setting out your argument.

Subject knowledge

1: Preliminary notes about grammar

Grammar involves the way in which words of different types are combined into sentences. The explanatory sections that follow will include definitions of types of word along with notes on how they are combined into sentences.

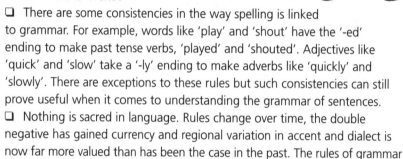

Three preliminary points about grammar:

❑ Function is all-important. Where a word is placed in relation to another word is crucial in deciding whether it is functioning as a verb or a noun. For example, the word 'run' will often be thought of as a verb. However, in a sentence like 'They went for a run', the word functions as a noun and the verb is 'went'.

❑ There are some consistencies in the way spelling is linked to grammar. For example, words like 'play' and 'shout' have the '-ed' ending to make past tense verbs, 'played' and 'shouted'. Adjectives like 'quick' and 'slow' take a '-ly' ending to make adverbs like 'quickly' and 'slowly'. There are exceptions to these rules but such consistencies can still prove useful when it comes to understanding the grammar of sentences.

❑ Nothing is sacred in language. Rules change over time, the double negative has gained currency and regional variation in accent and dialect is now far more valued than has been the case in the past. The rules of grammar that follow are subject to change as the language we use lives and grows.

2: Words and functions

Grammar picks out the functions of words. The major classes or types of word in the English language are:

noun

The name of something or someone, including concrete things, such as 'dog' or 'tree', and abstract things, such as 'happiness' or 'fear'.

pronoun

A word that replaces a noun. The noun 'John' in 'John is ill' can be replaced by a pronoun 'he', making 'He is ill'.

verb

A word that denotes an action or a happening. In the sentence 'I ate the cake' the verb is 'ate'. These are sometimes referred to as 'doing' words.

adjective

A word that modifies a noun. In the phrase 'the little boat' the adjective 'little' describes the noun 'boat'.

adverb
A word that modifies a verb. In the phrase 'he slowly walked' the adverb is 'slowly'.

preposition
A word or phrase that shows the relationship of one thing to another. In the phrase 'the house beside the sea' the preposition 'beside' places the two nouns in relation to each other.

conjunction
A word or phrase that joins other words and phrases. A simple example is the word 'and' that joins nouns in 'Snow White and Doc and Sneezy'.

article
The indefinite articles in English are 'a' and 'an' and the definite article is 'the'. Articles appear before nouns and denote whether the noun is specific ('give me the book') or not ('give me a book').

interjection
A word or phrase expressing or exclaiming an emotion, such as 'Oh!' and 'Aaargh!'

The various word types can be found in the following example sentences:

Lou	saw	his	new	house	from	the	train.
noun	verb	pronoun	adjective	noun	preposition	article	noun
Yeow!	I	hit	my	head	on	the	door.
interjection	pronoun	verb	pronoun	noun	preposition	article	noun
Amir	sadly	lost	his	bus fare	down	the	drain.
noun	adverb	verb	pronoun	noun	preposition	article	noun
Give	Jan	a	good	book	for	her	birthday.
verb	noun	article	adjective	noun	conjunction	pronoun	noun

The pages that follow provide more information on these word classes.

Nouns
There are four types of noun in English.

Common nouns are general names for things. For example, in the sentence 'I fed the dog', the noun 'dog' could be used to refer to any dog, not to a specific one. Other examples include 'boy', 'country', 'book', 'apple'.

Proper nouns are the specific names given to identify things or people. In a phrase like 'Sam is my dog' the word 'dog' is the common noun but 'Sam' is a proper noun because it refers to and identifies a specific dog. Other examples include 'the Prime Minister', 'Wales' and 'Amazing Grace'.

Collective nouns refer to a group of things together, such as 'a flock (of sheep)' or 'a bunch (of bananas)'.

A **noun** is the name of someone or something.

Abstract nouns refer to things that are not concrete, such as an action, a concept, an event, quality or state. Abstract nouns like 'happiness' and 'fulfilment' refer to ideas or feelings which are uncountable; others, such as 'hour', 'joke' and 'quantity' are countable.

Nouns can be singular or plural. To change a singular to a plural the usual rule is to add 's'. This table includes other rules to bear in mind, however:

If the singular ends in:	Rule	Examples
'y' after a consonant	Remove 'y', add 'ies'	party → parties
'y' after a vowel	add 's'	donkey → donkeys
'o' after a consonant	add 'es'	potato → potatoes
'o' after a vowel	add 's'	video → videos
a sound like 's', such as 's', 'sh', 'tch', 'x', 'z'	add 'es'	kiss → kisses dish → dishes watch → watches
'ch' sounding like it does at the end of 'perch'	add 'es'	church → churches

Pronouns

A **pronoun** is a word that stands in for a noun.

There are different classes of pronoun. The main types are:

Personal pronouns, referring to people or things, such as 'I', 'you', 'it'. The personal pronouns distinguish between subject and object case (I/me, he/him, she/her, we/us, they/them and the archaic thou/thee).

Reflexive pronouns, referring to people or things that are also the subject of the sentence. In the sentence 'You can do this yourself' the pronoun 'yourself' refers to 'you'. Such pronouns end with '-self' or '-selves'. Other examples include 'myself', 'themselves'.

Possessive pronouns identify people or things as belonging to a person or thing. For example, in the sentence 'The book is hers' the possessive pronoun 'hers' refers to 'the book'. Other examples include 'its' and 'yours'. Note that possessive pronouns never take an apostrophe.

Relative pronouns link relative clauses to their nouns. In the sentence 'The man who was in disguise sneaked into the room' the relative clause 'who was in disguise' provides extra information about 'the man'. This relative clause is linked by the relative pronoun 'who'. Other examples include 'whom', 'which' and 'that'.

Interrogative pronouns are used in questions. They refer to the thing that is being asked about. In the question 'What is your name?' and 'Where is the book?' the pronouns 'what' and 'where' stand for the answers – the name and the location of the book.

Demonstrative pronouns are pronouns that 'point'. They are used to show the relation of the speaker to an object. There are four demonstrative pronouns in English: 'this', 'that', 'these', 'those', used as in 'This is my house' and 'That is your house'. They have specific uses, depending upon the position of the object to the speaker:

	Near to speaker	Far away from speaker
Singular	this	that
Plural	these	those

Indefinite pronouns stand in for an indefinite noun. The indefinite element can be the number of elements or the nature of them but they are summed up in ambiguous pronouns such as 'any', 'some' or 'several'. Other examples are the pronouns that end with '-body', '-one' and '-thing', such as 'somebody', 'everyone' and 'anything'.

Person
Personal, reflexive and possessive pronouns can be in the first, second or third person.
First person pronouns (I, we) involve the speaker or writer.
Second person pronouns (you) refer to the listener or reader.
Third person pronouns refer to something other than these two participants in the communication (he, she, it, they).
The person of the pronoun will agree with particular forms of verbs: I like/ She likes.

Verbs
The **tense** of a verb places a happening in time. The main three tenses are the present, past and future.

A **verb** is a word that denotes an action or a happening.

To express an action that will take place in the future, verbs appear with 'will' or 'shall' (or 'going to'). The regular past tense is formed by the addition of the suffix '-ed', although some of the most common verbs in English (the 'strong' verbs) have irregular past tenses.

Present tense (happening now)	Past tense (happened in past)	Future tense (to happen in future)
am, say, find, kick	was, said, found, kicked	will be, will say, shall find, shall kick

Continuous verbs
The present participle form of a verb is used to show a continuous action. Whereas a past tense like 'kicked' denotes an action that happened ('I kicked'), the present participle denotes the action as happening and continuing as it is described ('I was kicking', the imperfect tense, or 'I am kicking', the present continuous). There is a sense in these uses of an action that has not ended.

The present participle usually ends in '-ing', such as 'walking', 'finding', and continuous verbs are made with a form of the verb 'be', such as 'was' or 'am': 'I was running' and 'I am running'.

Sometimes words look like verbs but are actually nouns.

Auxiliary verbs

Auxiliary verbs 'help' other verbs – they regularly accompany full verbs, always preceding them in a verb phrase. The auxiliary verbs in English can be divided into three categories:

Primary verbs are used to indicate the timing of a verb, such as 'be', 'have' or 'did' (including all their variations such as 'was', 'were', 'has', 'had' and so on). These can be seen at work in verb forms like 'I was watching a film', 'He has finished eating', 'I didn't lose my keys'.

Modal verbs indicate the possibility of an action occurring or the necessity of it happening, such as 'I might watch a film', 'I should finish eating' and 'I shouldn't lose my keys'. The modal verbs in English are: would, could, might, should, can, will, shall, may, and must. These verbs never function on their own as main verbs. They always act as auxiliaries helping other verbs.

Marginal modals, namely 'dare', 'need', 'ought to' and 'used to'. These act as modals, such as in the sentences 'I dared enter the room', 'You need to go away' and 'I ought to eat my dinner', but they can also act as main verbs, as in 'I need cake'.

Adjectives

An **adjective** is a word that modifies a noun.

The main function of adjectives is to define quality or quantity. Examples of the use of descriptions of quality include: 'good story', 'sad day' and 'stupid dog'. Examples of the use of descriptions of quantity include 'some stories', 'ten days' and 'many dogs'.

Adjectives can appear in one of three different degrees of intensity. In the table below it can be seen that there are '-er' and '-est' endings that show an adjective is comparative or superlative, though, as can be seen, there are exceptions. The regular comparative is formed by the addition of the suffix '-er' to shorter words and 'more' to longer words (kind/kinder, beautiful/more beautiful). The regular superlative is formed by the addition of the suffix '-est' to shorter words and 'most' to longer words. Note, however, that some common adjectives have irregular comparatives and superlatives.

Nominative	**Comparative**	**Superlative**
The nominative is the plain form that describes a noun.	The comparative implies a comparison between the noun and something else.	The superlative is the ultimate degree of a particular quality.
Examples	**Examples**	**Examples**
long	longer	longest
small	smaller	smallest
big	bigger	biggest
fast	faster	fastest
bad	worse	worst
good	better	best
far	farther/further	farthest/furthest

Adverbs

Adverbs provide extra information about the time, place or manner in which a verb happened.

Manner Provides information about the manner in which the action was done.	Ali *quickly* ran home. The cat climbed *fearfully* up the tree.
Time Provides information about the time at which the action occurred.	*Yesterday* Ali ran home. *Sometimes* the cat climbed up the tree.
Place Provides information about where the action took place.	*Outside* Ali ran home. *In the garden* the cat climbed up the tree.

An **adverb** is a word that modifies a verb.

Variations in the degree of intensity of an adverb are indicated by other adjectives such as 'very', 'rather', 'quite' and 'somewhat'. Comparative forms include 'very quickly', 'rather slowly', and 'most happily'.

The majority of single-word adverbs are made by adding '-ly' to an adjective: 'quick/quickly', 'slow/slowly' and so on.

Prepositions

Prepositions show how nouns or pronouns are positioned in relation to other nouns and pronouns in the same sentence. This can often be the location of one thing in relation to another in space, such as 'on', 'over', 'near'; or time, such as 'before', 'after'.

Prepositions are usually placed before a noun. They can consist of one word ('The cat *in* the tree...'), two words ('The cat *close to* the gate...') or three ('The cat *on top of* the roof...').

A **preposition** is a word or phrase that shows the relationship of one thing to another.

Conjunctions

Conjunctions can join words or clauses in one of four ways:

Name of conjunction	Nature of conjunction	Examples
Addition	One or more things together	We had our tea *and* went out to play. It was a cold day – *also* it rained.
Opposition	One or more things in opposition	I like coffee *but* my brother hates it. It could rain *or* it could snow.
Time	One or more things connected over time	Toby had his tea *then* went out to play. The bus left *before* we reached the stop.
Cause	One or more things causing or caused by another	I took a map *so that* we wouldn't get lost. We got lost *because* we had the wrong map.

A **conjunction** is a word or phrase that joins other words and phrases.

3: Understanding sentences
Types of sentence

The four main types of sentence are **declarative**, **interrogative**, **imperative** and **exclamatory**. The function of a sentence has an effect on the word order; imperatives, for example, often begin with a verb.

Sentence type	Function	Examples
Declarative	Makes a statement	The house is down the lane. Joe rode the bike.
Interrogative	Asks a question	Where is the house? What is Joe doing?
Imperative	Issues a command or direction	Turn left at the traffic lights. Get on your bike!
Exclamatory	Issues an interjection	Wow, what a mess! Oh no!

Sentences: Clauses and complexities
Phrases

A phrase is a set of words performing a grammatical function. In the sentence 'The little, old, fierce dog brutally chased the sad and fearful cat', there are three distinct units performing grammatical functions. The first phrase in this sentence essentially names the dog and provides descriptive information. This is a noun phrase, performing the job of a noun – 'the little, old, fierce dog'. To do this the phrase uses adjectives. The important thing to look out for is the way in which words build around a key word in a phrase. So here the words 'little', 'old' and 'fierce' are built around the word 'dog'. In examples like these, 'dog' is referred to as the **headword** and the adjectives are termed **modifiers**. Together, the modifier and headword make up the noun phrase. Modifiers can also come after the noun, as in 'The little, old, fierce dog that didn't like cats brutally chased the sad and fearful cat'. In this example 'little, 'old' and 'fierce' are **premodifiers** and the phrase 'that didn't like cats' is a **postmodifier**.

The noun phrase is just one of the types of phrase that can be made.

Phrase type	Examples
Noun phrase	The *little, old fierce dog* didn't like cats. She gave him *a carefully and colourfully covered book*.
Verb phrase	The dog *had been hiding* in the house. The man *climbed through* the window without a sound.
Adjectival phrase	The floor was *completely clean*. The floor was *so clean you could eat your dinner off it*.
Adverbial phrase	I finished my lunch *very slowly indeed*. *More confidently than usual*, she entered the room.
Prepositional phrase	The cat sat *at the top of* the tree. The phone rang *in the middle of* the night.

Notice that phrases can appear within phrases. A noun phrase like 'carefully and colourfully covered book' contains the adjectival phrase 'carefully and colourfully covered'. This string of words forms the adjectival phrase in which the words 'carefully' and 'colourfully' modify the adjective 'covered'. Together these words 'carefully and colourfully covered' modify the noun 'book', creating a distinct noun phrase. This is worth noting as it shows how the boundaries between phrases can be blurred, a fact that can cause confusion unless borne in mind!

Clauses

Clauses are units of meaning included within a sentence, usually containing a verb and other elements linked to it. 'The burglar ran' is a clause containing the definite article, noun and verb; 'The burglar quickly ran from the little house' is also a clause that adds an adverb, preposition and adjective. The essential element in a clause is the verb. Clauses look very much like small sentences, indeed sentences can be constructed of just one clause: 'The burglar hid', 'I like cake'.

Sentences can also be constructed out of a number of clauses linked together: 'The burglar ran and I chased him because he stole my cake.' This sentence contains three clauses: 'The burglar ran', 'I chased him', 'he stole my cake'.

Clauses and phrases: the difference

Clauses include participants in an action denoted by a verb. Phrases, however, need not necessarily contain a verb. These phrases make little sense on their own: 'without a sound', 'very slowly indeed'. They work as part of a clause.

Simple, compound and complex sentences

The addition of clauses can make complex or compound sentences.

Simple sentences are made up of one clause, for example: 'The dog barked', 'Sam was scared'.

Compound sentences are made up of clauses added to clauses. In compound sentences each of the clauses is of equal value; no clause is dependent on another. An example of a compound sentence is: 'The dog barked and the parrot squawked'. Both these clauses are of equal importance: 'The dog barked', 'the parrot squawked'.

Other compound sentences include, for example: 'I like coffee and I like chocolate', 'I like coffee, but I don't like tea'.

Complex sentences are made up of a main clause with a subordinate clause or clauses. Subordinate clauses make sense in relation to the main clause. They say something about it and are dependent upon it, for example in the sentences: 'The dog barked because he saw a burglar', 'Sam was scared so he phoned the police'.

In both these cases the subordinate clause ('he saw a burglar', 'he phoned the police') is elaborating on the main clause. They explain why the dog barked or why Sam was scared and, in doing so, are subordinate to those actions. The reader needs to see the main clauses to fully appreciate what the subordinate ones are stating.

Subject and object

The **subject** of a sentence or clause is the agent that performs the action denoted by the verb – '*Shaun* threw the ball'. The **object** is the agent to which the verb is done – 'ball'. It could be said that the subject does the verb to the object (a simplification but a useful one). The simplest type of sentence is known as the SVO (subject–verb–object) sentence (or clause), as in 'You lost your way', 'I found the book' and 'Lewis met Chloe'.

The active voice and the passive voice

These contrast two ways of saying the same thing:

Active voice	Passive voice
I found the book. Megan met Ben. The cow jumped over the moon.	The book was found by me. Ben was met by Megan. The moon was jumped over by the cow.

The two types of clause put the same subject matter in a different **voice**. Passive clauses are made up of a subject and verb followed by an agent.

The book	was found by	me.
subject	verb	agent
Ben	was met by	Megan.
subject	verb	agent

Sentences can be written in the active or the passive voice. A sentence can be changed from the active to the passive voice by:

❑ moving the subject to the end of the clause
❑ moving the object to the start of the clause
❑ changing the verb or verb phrase by placing a form of the verb 'be' before it (as in 'was found')
❑ changing the verb or verb phrase by placing 'by' after it.

In passive clauses the agent can be deleted, either because it does not need mentioning or because a positive choice is made to omit it. Texts on science may leave out the agent, with sentences such as 'The water is added to the salt and stirred'.

4: Punctuation

Punctuation provides marks within sentences that guide the reader. Speech doesn't need punctuation (and would sound bizarre if it included noises for full stops etc). In speech, much is communicated by pausing, changing tone and so on. In writing, the marks within and around a sentence provide indications of when to pause, when something is being quoted and so on.

Punctuation mark	Uses	Examples
A	**Capital letter** 1. Start a sentence. 2. Indicate proper nouns. 3. Emphasize certain words.	All I want is cake. You can call me Al. I want it TOMORROW!
•	**Full stop** Ends sentences that are not questions or exclamations.	This is a sentence.
?	**Question mark** Ends a sentence that is a question.	Is this a question?
!	**Exclamation mark** Ends a sentence that is an exclamation.	Don't do that!
" " ' '	**Quotation (speech) marks (or inverted commas)** Enclose direct speech. Can be double or single.	"Help me," the man yelled. 'Help me,' the man yelled.
,	**Comma** 1. Places a pause between clauses within a sentence. 2. Separates items in a list. 3. Separates adjectives in a series. 4. Completely encloses clauses inserted in a sentence. 5. Marks speech from words denoting who said them.	We were late, although it didn't matter. You will need eggs, butter, salt and flour. I wore a long, green, frilly skirt. We were, after we had rushed to get there, late for the film. 'Thank you,' I said.
-	**Hyphen** Connects elements of certain words.	Co-ordinator, south-west.
:	**Colon** 1. Introduces lists (including examples).	To go skiing these are the main items you will need: a hat, goggles, gloves and sunscreen.

continued...

Punctuation mark	Uses	Examples
	2. Introduces summaries. 3. Introduces (direct) quotations. 4. Introduces a second clause that expands or illustrates the meaning of the first.	We have learned the following on the ski slope: do a snow plough to slow down… My instructor always says: 'Bend those knees.' The snow hardened: it turned into ice.
;	**Semicolon** 1. Separates two closely linked clauses, and shows there is a link between them. 2. Separates items in a complex list.	On Tuesday, the bus was late; the train was early. You can go by aeroplane, train and taxi; Channel tunnel train, coach, then a short walk; or aeroplane and car.
'	**Apostrophe of possession** Denotes the ownership of one thing by another (see page 160).	This is Mona's scarf. These are the teachers' books.
'	**Apostrophe of contraction** Shows the omission of a letter(s) when two (or occasionally more) words are contracted.	Don't walk on the grass.
•••	**Ellipsis** 1. Shows the omission of words. 2. Indicates a pause.	The teacher moaned, 'Look at this floor… a mess… this class…' Lou said: 'I think I locked the door… no, hang on, did I?'
( )	**Brackets** Contains a parenthesis – a word or phrase added to a sentence to give a bit more information.	The cupboard (which had been in my family for years) was broken.
—	**Dash** 1. Indicates additional information, with more emphasis than a comma. 2. Indicates a pause, especially for effect at the end of a sentence. 3. Contains extra information (used instead of brackets).	She is a teacher – and a very good one too. We all know what to expect – the worst. You finished that job – and I don't know how – before the deadline.

Adding an apostrophe of possession

The addition of an apostrophe can create confusion. The main thing to look at is the noun – ask:

❑ Is it singular or plural?
❑ Does it end in an 's'?

If the noun is singular and doesn't end in 's', you add an apostrophe and an 's', for example: Indra's house the firefighter's bravery	If the noun is singular and ends in 's', you add an apostrophe and an 's', for example: the bus's wheels Thomas's pen
If the noun is plural and doesn't end in 's', you add an apostrophe and an 's', for example: the women's magazine the geese's flight	If the noun is plural and ends in 's', you add an apostrophe but don't add an 's', for example: the boys' clothes the dancers' performance

Further reading

Carter, R; Goddard, A; Reah, D; Sanger, K; Bowring, K (1997) *Working with Texts: A Core Book for Language Analysis*, Routledge

Crystal, D (1988) *Rediscover Grammar with David Crystal*, Longman

Crystal, D (1995) *The Cambridge Encyclopedia of the English Language*, Cambridge University Press
A big volume but very accessible, covering many areas of English including grammar, punctuation and dialect. Filled with interesting asides and examples from sources as varied as Shakespeare to Monty Python.

Hurford, R (1994) *Grammar: A student's guide*, Cambridge University Press
An excellent text, setting out basic guidelines on the workings of grammar.

Reah, D and Ross, A (1997) *Exploring Grammar: Main Routes and Scenic Paths*, WordsWork
A popular and accessible introductory course to grammar with interesting exercises to guide the reader.

Sealey, A (1996) *Learning About Language: Issues for Primary Teachers*, Open University Press
A more theoretical work that presents some of the issues and arguments surrounding knowledge about language.